TEXAS
HISTORIC
INNS
COOKBOOK

TEXAS
HISTORIC
INNS
COOKBOOK

by
ANN RUFF AND GAIL DRAGO

★
TexasMonthlyPress

Texas Monthly Press, Inc.
P. O. Box 1569
Austin, Texas 78767

A   B   C   D   E   F   G   H

Library of Congress Cataloging in Publication Data

Ruff, Ann, 1930-
      Texas historic inns cookbook.

      Includes index.
      1. Cookery—Texas.   2. Cookery, International
3. Hotels, taverns, etc.—Texas.   4. Historic buildings—
Texas.   I. Drago, Gail, 1947-   II. Title.
TX715.R9263   1985   641.5'09764   84-24019
ISBN 0-932012-45-0

To Barbara Rodriguez, who showed me the way, and to John Hamilton, Susan Pryor, and Delores Keller, who cooked and cooked and cooked and cooked.

—Ann Ruff

To Anthony Drago, for giving me the freedom to write, and to my father and inspiration, Rousseaux Constantine, whose kingdom was his kitchen.

—Gail Drago

Acknowledgments

First and foremost, we would like to thank all the historic inn-keepers, managers, food and beverage directors, and public relations representatives who sent us their wonderful recipes. They patiently answered every tedious question that was necessary to perfect these treasures. This was quite a chore, since most of the recipes had never been written down but had been stored for years in the minds of Texas's greatest cooks. We would also like to thank all those hotel owners who so graciously entertained us so we could experience their food and hospitality firsthand. Our gratitude also goes to our dear friend and consultant, Peter Morris, whose guidance and support spurred us to this pursuit.

To our friends who were good enough to help us test all these recipes, we couldn't have done it without you. Thanks go also to Waverly Constantine, the Bill Neil clan, Johnny Lewallen, and Bonnie and Alan Crawford, who "kept the home fires burning" for Gail so she could do her research and to Carlo and Mamie Drago for helping us lick an untold number of stamps and envelopes. In addition, we want to thank Michael Earney for his illustrations, which have added visual excitement to our book.

Special thanks go to Sylvia Lewallen and Faith Clotiaux, who out of love typed more than one hundred pages of manuscript in three days' time. Their "blood, sweat, and tears" stain this text.

Appreciation goes also to Anthony and Nicholas Drago, who agreed to taste even the most questionable concoctions and especially to Anthony, who took so much time away from his canvas to help us finish this project.

And we certainly don't want to forget all the tasters who shared in our experiments. Their comments added so much to the *Texas Historic Inns Cookbook*.

Table of Contents

Introduction

This book is much more than just delicious recipes to tempt the appetite. It is also a trip back in time to an era filled with romance. Even if the recipes are modern, the settings may be antebellum, Victorian, or from the exciting 1920s.

Until the 1950s, hotels were the hub of a community's activities, and most social events revolved around their reception rooms and banquet halls. A hotel was much more than just a place to stay; it was a tradition. No two looked alike. Each had its own special decor and even possessed a distinct personality. The opulent Adolphus had its own aura, while the historic Menger had its status. Many hotels depended on the trains for their existence, and "drummers" (as traveling salesmen were called, since they "drummed up business") provided a great deal of their trade. Then the interstate highways bypassed towns, airports replaced train stations, and shopping malls moved to the suburbs. Grand traditional hotels were left behind to become grimy, rotting hulks.

But throughout the United States and Texas today there is a vibrant resurgence of nostalgia. Many factors have contributed to this yearning for the past, but a definite group of travelers now search for antique buildings, antique furnishings, and antique atmosphere. Fortunately, Texas has another wonderful group of people: those who have restored historic hotels for guests to enjoy once again. Most of the restorations have included a restaurant with the same ambience as the hotel. Few of the menus go back to the era of the hotel; but no matter how modern the fare may be, the surroundings make it a very special dining experience.

The stories and histories of the inns and hotels are as unique as Texas itself. No matter how large or how small the establishment, the owners and chefs of these historic hotels are delighted to share their favorite recipes and their origin with you. Some dishes are treasured family heirlooms, others are traditional Texas favorites, and some chefs have contributed the latest in nouvelle cuisine. Each contribution came to us because guests found this recipe particularly delectable. Each contribution was also submitted in the sincere belief that visitors will want to dine in the original setting and share the old-fashioned hospitality of all of these grand old hotels.

The Adolphus
Dallas

Deep in the heart of Texas sits a grand *dame du monde*. She is the Adolphus, dressed in Renaissance finery and schooled in the art of southern hospitality. Her very existence is proof that Texas was and is the place where dreams can come true, as they did for Adolphus Busch, the creator of his own namesake hotel.

The Busch story is a common one in Texas. Adolphus was a young man with the wild idea to ship Budweiser, his famous beer, out of state from St. Louis to Texas in the new refrigerated railroad cars. Of course, his idea was a great one, and Texans have been drinking Budweiser ever since. To thank Dallas, as well as the state of Texas, for accepting him, he decided to build the grandest building "west of Venice, Italy."

And grand it is, all twenty-one red brick and granite stories decorated with stone carvings, gargoyles, and bronze mythological figures and capped with a stylized representation of a giant beer bottle. Louis XV would have loved the interior grillwork, marble trim, and art from the French Renaissance period. The restored chandeliers that hang in the lobby and registration area are a pair commissioned by Busch for exhibition at the 1904 World's Fair in St. Louis. These masterpieces are particularly significant, adorned as they are with eagles, Budweiser's trademark. Busch's love of his company product is also seen in the use of hops that adorn the eight marbleized columns in the French Room.

The original hotel was filled with such treasures, and apparently Westgroup, Inc., and the New England Mutual Life Insurance Company saw all this when they decided to purchase it in 1981. The two companies brought the Adolphus to its fullest potential by spending $45 million to restore it. The number of rooms was reduced from more than 800 to 439, giving the hotel some of the largest guest rooms in Dallas. There are 18 luxurious suites that range up to 2,400 square feet, some with outdoor terraces and others with large rooftop skylights. All room furnishings are custom-made Chippendale and Queen Anne styles. Doors have Williamsburg paneling. The designers succeeded in keeping the

1

Old World motif even with the guest rooms. As a result of this fusion of the old with the new, the Adolphus is now one of the most beautiful American hotels in the Old World tradition.

The new Adolphus, filled with original artwork from all over the world, is an artist's dream. Of the Louis XV and XVI collection, Jill Kertin, the hotel's chief designer, says that "it is probably the finest in quality and quantity to be seen in any hotel in America." Extremely valuable, the collection includes a huge nineteenth-century French portrait of Napoleon Bonaparte. The most interesting work, however, can be found in the elegant French Room, which is one of the three restaurants added during the hotel's revival. Adolphus himself would have been proud to see what was done to "his finest jewel" during renovation. To keep the eighteenth-century motif, artists assembled by Peter Wolf Concepts of Dallas painted murals of pastoral lovers surrounded by blue skies that are full of flower-carrying cherubs and white billowy clouds. Scenic designer James Frazer and his muralists painted the vaulted ceilings on their backs atop scaffolding as Michelangelo did in the Vatican's Sistine Chapel. The huge ceiling of the grand ballroom is painted in the same Rococo style with clouds, lyres, horns, drums, mandolins, violins, and sheet music.

To find paradise, go to the French Room and order from fifty menu choices in the classical French and nouvelle cuisines, including such delicacies as sautéed pigeon garnished with liver and garlic mousse, Beluga caviar, duck consommé with ginger, or goose livers in aspic and brioches. The food is absolutely superb; how could it not be, with the celebrated chef Jean Banchet as consultant to the Adolphus in the preparation and serving of dishes? The owner of Le Français in the Chicago suburb of Wheeling, Chef Banchet has been associated with renowned restaurants and hotels in France, Monte Carlo, and London. His Le Français has been rated by critics as the best restaurant in America. Executive chefs of the French Room are Pascal Gode and Pascal Vignau, both trained in France. To acquaint themselves with Banchet's wishes and procedures, they each spent a month at Le Français observing its operation.

If you're just in the mood for tea, the afternoon ritual of high tea in the main lobby is patterned after fashionable European hotels. High tea offers a variety of famous teas, old ports and sherries, cappuccinos, finger sandwiches, petit fours, and homemade ice creams and sherbets. The service and background piano music are excellent.

For a more formal setting, have a drink in the French Room bar next to the fireplace. The hearth is made of Belgian black marble and the overmantel of English Chippendale mahogany. Note also the authentic seventeenth-, eighteenth-, and nineteenth-century antiques. For a touch of New York, lounge in the Palm Bar, a stylish New York pub with sofa-like booths divided by a sandblasted end-lit glass burgundy marble and oak bar. A beautifully executed Portuguese tile mural of botanical prints of palms decorates this classy bar, which serves cuisine for the busy shopper or executive. If you feel like eating light, the Grille offers a variety of food, such as soups, salads, and fresh steamed vegetables. Fresh-baked breads, rolls, croissants, brioches, and Danish pastries are also offered. For a more complete meal, there are seafoods, duckling, lamb, and steaks prepared in the American or classical traditions, along with quiche and unusual desserts.

If you're in Dallas, put this hotel first on your list of things to do. Described as "the beautiful lady with a past," the Adolphus provides a graceful sanctuary from the hustle and bustle of today's world.

Calf's Liver with Raspberry Vinegar

Serves 2

Liver seems to be one of the few meats that no one is wishy-washy about. You either love it or can't stand it. For those liver lovers, the Adolphus's executive chef, Gerard Bahon, prepares this unusual recipe.

8 ounces calf's liver
4 tablespoons butter
1 tablespoon shallots, chopped
1 ounce raspberry vinegar
2 ounces brown sauce
Salt and pepper to taste
1 tablespoon parsley, chopped

Sauté liver very quickly in 2 tablespoons butter. When liver is done to your taste, reserve. Remove most of the fat from the skillet. Sauté shallots and deglaze with vinegar. Let the liquid reduce, and add brown sauce. Let cook until sauce obtains the desired consistency. Whisk in the rest of the butter and the parsley. Salt and pepper to taste. Pour very hot sauce over liver.

Oysters with White Leek Sauce

Serves 1

6 oysters
2 shallots, chopped
¼ cup white wine
½ cup cream
4 leeks — white only, julienne
Salt and pepper to taste

Open oysters, reserve shallow halves, and heat oyster meat just until warm. Do not cook it. Sauté shallots very quickly, then add white wine. Let liquid reduce to half. When ready, pour in cream and let reduce until sauce coats back of spoon. Then put leeks in sauce. Let them simmer for about 20 seconds. Salt and pepper to taste.

Put oyster meat in shell and pour sauce with leeks on top of oysters. Serve very hot.

Dark Chocolate Truffles

Yields 9 dozen

1 pint whipping cream
½ cup granulated sugar
10 ounces semisweet chocolate *plus*
10 ounces semisweet chocolate for coating
Cocoa powder

Bring the whipping cream to a boil and add sugar. Stir in 10 ounces of chocolate until dissolved, but thick like a sauce. Refrigerate covered for 1 hour or until really cold. Remove from the refrigerator and stir chocolate mixture over hot water until it reaches room temperature. As it loses its chill, it becomes elastic and will not pour from a spoon. Drop from a teaspoon in uniform, walnut-sized bits on a tray covered with foil or waxed paper. Refrigerate 30 minutes; roll in cocoa powder and return to the refrigerator.

To coat: Melt remaining semisweet chocolate over hot water. Remove truffles from the refrigerator and dip in melted chocolate to make a shell. Roll in cocoa powder again. These will keep in the refrigerator about two weeks.

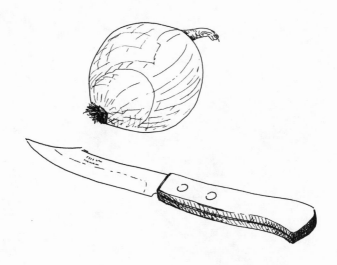

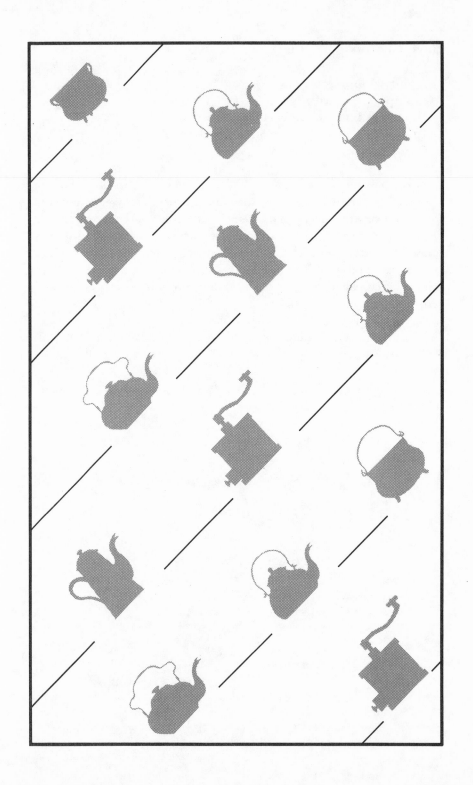

Ambassador
Park
Hotel
Dallas

The Ambassador Park Hotel has had many different faces, names, and owners since its birth in 1905, but its stately elegance has remained steadfast all these years. Today it has finally come into its own, restored in such a way as to show off its historic beauty, and dressed in finery fit for a statesman. The new owners, the Texas Management Company and TAP Historical Properties, opened the grand old doors again in December 1982, giving back to Dallas still another historic hotel. The amenities are certainly present, waiting to be lavished on the most princely or the most humble guests. You couldn't ask for more, with a butler on every floor who sees to your every wish, an intricate telephone system in every room that does everything but make your executive decisions for you (your private line can also be hooked up to your company computer), and your own special nightcap served at turndown. Chocolates are expertly made on each floor by the butlers, who also act as tour guides, tailors, handymen, and servants.

And the food? It's nothing short of sensational, with fresh seafood flown in daily from Louisiana to landlocked Dallas. The cuisine varies from continental to French nouvelle to creole (probably because the general manager, Bill Besson, has roots in Louisiana and knows the true meaning of *bon appétit*).

As for the Ambassador's past, there is plenty of it. Its beginnings go back to around the turn of the century, when the Majestic Apartment Building Company purchased a plot of land from local businessman C. H. Alexander in 1903. At that time, the property was part of the then-fashionable Cedars neighborhood. The company then began constructing the Majestic Hotel with local architect Earl Henry Silven at the helm. The result was a Dallas version of the popular Sullivanesque style, distinguished by Georgian gables and balustraded roof ornamentation. When it opened in 1905, the Majestic was proclaimed the city's premier hotel. Such greats as Theodore Roosevelt, William Howard Taft, Woodrow Wilson, and even Sarah Bernhardt honored the hotel with their presence.

The Majestic was alive with constant activity. Local papers were always covering stories of social activities such as the Idlewilde Ball. The *Dallas Morning News* reported, "The ballroom was resplendent in the Club's colors. . . . The center pillar represented a birch tree. . . . An orchestra of 28 pieces was stationed on the balcony."

Only a year later, the hotel went into receivership, and it became the Park Hotel. By 1910 the future began to look brighter for the old Majestic. Multimillionairess Electra Waggoner Wharton, of the prominent Fort Worth Waggoner family, purchased the hotel. After she spent $50,000 on its revitalization, Electra lost the Park to her husband, A. B., in a divorce settlement. Other investors saved the hotel from the wrecking ball, but it was not until 1981 that the Park regained its former glory.

Now a Texas historic landmark, a Dallas historic landmark, and a candidate for the National Register of Historic Places, the Ambassador Park Hotel provides guests with 118 rooms; 80 of them are suites. All rooms are individually decorated with period reproductions, plush carpet, wet bars restocked daily, and graceful, original archways. The color scheme is vibrant, with alternating floors in burgundies and pinks or shades of green.

The Ambassador Park Restaurant, with its Chippendale furnishings, ivory tablecloths, and rich blue booths and carpets, is a lovely spot to share a meal. The adjoining piano-bar lounge adds dinner music and an air of informality to this comfortable formal setting. The exquisite rosewood grand piano is of pre–Civil War vintage and a beautiful centerpiece to the lounge. Plans are also being made to build an upbeat jazz bar in the basement featuring local musicians.

All the furnishings in the lobby, hallways, and the mezzanine are restored and original to the building. In addition, the elevator to the east of the lobby, still in good working order, is claimed to be the oldest west of the Mississippi. The 1933 white facade with its red tile roof is unchanged except for additions of dark green awnings.

The Ambassador Park Hotel has all of the charm and ambience of a fine European hotel. The service is impeccable, the accommodations luxurious, and the cuisine excellent. The Ambassador Park has accomplished all of these and still preserves a big part of Dallas's history.

Steak Le Rouge

Serves 2

1 stick of butter or margarine, melted
2 tablespoons lemon juice
5 tablespoons green onions, chopped
2 to 4 ounces crabmeat (optional)
2 filet mignons

Combine butter, lemon juice, green onions, and crabmeat in heavy skillet. Cook steaks to desired degree of doneness in mixture. Top with Sauce Béarnaise.

Sauce Bearnaise
3 shallots or scallions, finely chopped
1 teaspoon tarragon or 1 tablespoon fresh tarragon, chopped
¼ cup white wine
¼ cup wine vinegar (red or white)
1 teaspoon chopped fresh parsley
Basic hollandaise sauce recipe (packaged mix is acceptable)

Combine shallots, tarragon, wine, wine vinegar, and parsley. Bring to a boil and reduce to practically a glaze. Add this to basic hollandaise. If tarragon is fresh, it is sometimes pleasant to stir in an extra dash or two.

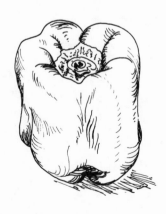

Pain à la Bourbon

Serves 4 to 6

1 quart whole milk
3 eggs
14 ounces sugar
4 tablespoons cinnamon
2 tablespoons nutmeg
1 18-inch loaf French bread
1 cup raisins

Mix first five ingredients together in large mixing bowl. Cut French bread in 1-inch slices and add to mixture. Add raisins and mix above items together. Pour mixture into a greased shallow pan, which has been placed in a larger pan with water to prevent mixture from sticking. Bake at 350° until knife comes out clean when inserted, approximately 30 to 40 minutes.

Sauce
1 stick butter
2 egg yolks
7 ounces sugar
3–4 ounces bourbon

Melt butter. Add egg yolks and sugar. Stir sauce to a smooth texture. Add bourbon to taste while blending. When pudding is done, let cool. Serve by scooping or slicing to portion size. Ladle sauce over pudding.

Annie's Bed and Breakfast
Big Sandy

If you are wondering where Big Sandy is, take U.S. Highway 80 east out of Dallas. You'll go through Wills Point and pass the Salt Palace in Grand Saline. If you reach Gladewater, turn back. You've missed Big Sandy by about ten miles. When you turn north off Highway 80 in Big Sandy, don't be surprised if you can hardly maneuver your car among all the chartered buses. The parking lots are jammed, the place is literally a mob of people, and the reasons for all this activity are three houses decked out in bright paint and gingerbread trim. This is Annie's Bed and Breakfast, but Annie is offering a lot more than just bed and breakfast.

None of the three houses is a Texas landmark, and all have been extensively remodeled, but all are absolutely wonderful. The actual bed and breakfast house is furnished in lovely antiques, handmade quilts, brass beds, and real Victorian charm. It is difficult to tour all the rooms, for this is a very popular inn, and reservations should be made well in advance.

If you cannot spend the night, you can dine in the restaurant in a turn-of-the-century atmosphere on lots of delicious homemade dishes. Flowered wallpaper, lace tablecloths, and waitresses in housemaid uniforms create the genteel atmosphere so dear to Victorian ladies' hearts.

Annie's is world-famous for handcrafted items. Everything you ever wanted to crochet, knit, needlepoint, crewel, quilt, or embroider is for sale at Annie's. Or you can buy your own kit, sharpen your needles, and fashion your own masterpiece. One entire house is filled with beautiful crafts, sort of "do-it-yourself antiques."

11

Italian Coconut Cake

Yields 1 12 x 9-inch layer

1 stick margarine
½ cup shortening
5 egg yolks
2 cups sugar
2 cups flour
1 teaspoon soda
1 cup buttermilk
1 can coconut
1 cup nuts, chopped
5 egg whites, stiffly beaten
1 teaspoon vanilla

Cream margarine and shortening; add egg yolks, sugar, flour, and soda, alternating with buttermilk. Beat until smooth. Add coconut and nuts. Fold in egg whites and vanilla. Bake in 12 x 9-inch cake pan 20 minutes at 250°.

Frosting
5 tablespoons flour
1 cup milk
1 cup sugar
1 cup margarine
1 teaspoon vanilla
Coconut

Combine flour and milk and cook on low heat until thick, stirring constantly. Cool. Cream sugar, margarine, and vanilla. Add flour mixture and beat until creamy and of consistency to spread. Sprinkle coconut on top and sides of cake after frosting.

Stuffed French Toast

Yields 10 to 12 slices

1 8-ounce package cream cheese, softened
¼ cup crushed pineapple
½ cup pecans, chopped
1 16-ounce loaf French bread
4 eggs
1 cup whipping cream
½ teaspoon vanilla
1 teaspoon ground nutmeg
1 12-ounce jar (1½ cups) apricot preserves
½ cup orange juice

Beat cream cheese and pineapple together until fluffy. Stir in nuts; set aside. Cut bread into 10 to 12 1½-inch slices; cut a pocket in the top of each. Fill each with 1½ tablespoons of the cheese mixture. Beat together eggs, whipping cream, vanilla, and nutmeg. Using tongs, dip the filled bread slices in egg mixture, being careful not to squeeze out the filling. Cook on lightly greased griddle until both sides are golden brown. Meanwhile, heat together preserves and juice. To serve, drizzle apricot mixture over hot French toast.

Badu
House
Llano

When you first see the Badu House, this stern, imposing brick and granite building may not be how you imagined a country inn to look. That is because it was originally built in 1891 as the First National Bank of Llano. The builders probably hoped that its stern facade would inspire trust and confidence in Llano's citizens. The trust and confidence only lasted until 1898, when the bank failed and the building was sold at auction to N. J. Badu. Always known as "Prof," this French entrepreneur made the building a home for his wife and two girls.

Badu and his descendants lived in the house for more than eighty years. Already placed on the National Register of Historic Places and a Texas historical landmark when Ann and the late Earl Ruff purchased it in 1980, the Badu House began another era as a country inn.

The exterior of the Badu House is unchanged and still a solid block of brick with its unique granite checkerboard trim, but when you open the heavy doors with their beautiful stained-glass panels, you are transported back to great-grandmother's life and times. Victorian wallpaper in shades of blue and pink takes your breath away with its striking patterns, and bric-a-brac and old photographs add numerous touches of charm. "Prof" himself beams down from a portrait over the fireplace, no doubt quite pleased with his home's elegant transformation.

Upstairs, oak panels that separated lawyers' offices in 1891 now line the hallway for eight charming guest rooms and seven baths for overnight guests. Furnished in antiques, collectibles, and funky wallpaper, the rooms offer a delightful return to the past.

One of the most beautiful features of the Badu House is the bar in the Llanite Club. Hearty drinks are served on slabs of polished llanite, a rare opaline mineral with large blue quartz crystals that sparkle in the sunlight. Llanite is found only in Llano County, and this may be the largest display of this unusual stone in the world.

The Badu House menu is fairly limited yet appeals to a variety of palates. Ann has contributed her specialties with Ann's Chicken, Badu

House potatoes, and cornbread crepes. Maggie Currie, the manager (and sometimes the night cook), has contributed her marvelous shrimp scampi, which is a favorite with dinner guests.

For lunch, the Badu House kitchen is presided over by Angelita Najar, and her deft hands work miracles with dough, desserts, and Mexican specialties such as empanadas, chiles rellenos, enchiladas, and chalupas. She also cooks a fine chicken-fried steak and brews up a heavenly beef stew.

All of these tasty morsels are served by waitresses in Victorian housemaid costumes as you dine on blue tablecloths with cut glassware and gleaming silverplate. At the Badu House you can enjoy the ambience of the past with delicious food, excellent service, and a grand old historic building.

Ann's Chicken

Serves 6

Before the Badu House was ready for guests, I fantasized about the many gourmet dishes I would serve in the lovely Victorian dining rooms. Llano and its environs would be delighted and enchanted with the unique fare, and I would soon be the rage of the Hill Country. Having never been in the restaurant business before, I had no concept of how different it is to cook commercially from those charming little dinner parties in my home. Well, Llano and the environs simply refused to order my exquisite spinach salad, zesty gazpacho, or delicate omelets. It was a steak-and-potato world out there, and I found myself starving to death in a kitchen full of food.

Now my menu consists of a great hamburger, a super chicken-fried steak, and Angelita's Mexican food at lunch. Dinner gives you a choice of two excellent steaks, Mississippi catfish, baked potatoes, and fried shrimp. However, one gourmet dish stuck to the stomachs of Llano and has endured as a real bestseller on the dinner menu — Ann's Chicken.

12 boned and skinned chicken breasts
24 thin jalapeño slices, seeds removed
1 pound bacon
1 large cooking bag
1 cup chopped pimentos
1 medium-sized bottle Italian dressing

Spread chicken breasts flat. Place 2 jalapeño slices in each breast. Roll up breast and wrap with one bacon slice. Place in lightly floured cooking bag. Bag should be spread out in shallow baking pan. Sprinkle chicken with chopped pimentos and cover with Italian dressing. Seal bag and marinate overnight in refrigerator.

When ready to bake, puncture bag and bake 1 hour at 350°. Serve two chicken breasts per person on bed of fluffy rice.

Extras

A small slice of Monterey Jack cheese with the jalapeño slices is an added touch you may wish to try.

The unused portion of this dish can be frozen in its marinade and loses none of its flavor when reheated.

Mexican Chicken Casserole

Serves 8

When it comes to Mexican specialties, you can search all over Texas and not find better Mexican food than Angelita Najar's renditions.

1 (3½-pound) broiler-fryer
2 tablespoons butter or margarine
1 medium onion, chopped
1 green pepper, chopped
1 teaspoon garlic salt
1 can (10½ ounces) cream of mushroom soup, undiluted
½ cup plus 2 tablespoons canned tomatoes
½ cup plus 2 tablespoons canned green chilies
1½ dozen corn tortillas
2 cups shredded cheddar cheese

Place chicken in a Dutch oven; add enough water to cover chicken. Bring to a boil; cover and simmer 1 hour or until chicken is tender. Remove chicken from oven and reserve 1 cup broth. Debone chicken and cut into bite-sized pieces. Set aside.

Melt butter in a skillet; add onion, green pepper, and garlic salt. Sauté until tender.

In a large bowl combine onion mixture, soup, reserved chicken broth, tomatoes, and green chilies. Mix well.

Tear tortillas into bite-sized pieces; place half the tortilla pieces in a greased 13 x 9 x 2-inch baking dish. Top with half of soup mixture, and then add half of diced chicken. Sprinkle with half of cheese. Repeat layers. Bake at 350° uncovered for 30 minutes (or until bubbly).

Tortilla-Wrapped Chiles Rellenos

Serves 5

Every Wednesday night at the Badu House you have your choice of Mexican food or chicken-fried steak. Yes, every lunch has a Mexican plate and a chicken-fried steak, too, but on Wednesday nights the chicken-fried covers the plate, and Angelita adds a Mexican gourmet treat to her refried beans, enchiladas, and tacos — her stuffed chiles rellenos. Both meals are Llano favorites, and often couples order one of each and split them, thereby getting the best of both worlds. Wednesdays are long days for Angelita, but all of her Mexican food is prepared fresh. Nothing frozen ever comes out on Angelita's Mexican plates.

3 4-ounce cans whole green chilies
10 ounces cheddar cheese
10 large flour tortillas (10-inch diameter)
½ cup milk
1 egg
1 cup Pillsbury's Best All-Purpose or Unbleached Flour
2 teaspoons chili powder
½ teaspoon garlic salt
Oil for deep frying
Salsa picante

Separate chilies to make 10 individual pieces. Slice cheese into 10 strips and place inside chilies. Place a cheese-stuffed chili in center of each tortilla. Fold ends of tortilla over chili, envelope-style, and secure with toothpicks.

In small bowl, beat milk and egg until blended. In another bowl, combine flour, chili powder, and garlic salt. Dip tortilla in egg mixture, then coat with flour mixture. Fry in deep fat in heavy saucepan for approximately 2 minutes on each side until golden brown.

Serve with salsa picante.

Sam Oatman's Rio Llano Chili

Serves 4 to 6

The Oatmans have been around Llano ever since there was a Llano to be around — about 1844, to be exact. And there has been an Oatman lawyer in Llano since then as well. Sam is carrying on the family tradition and spends a lot of time stamping out injustice. But in Sam's next life he will probably come back as a country-and-western superstar, for he loves to sing and play his guitar.

The Llanite Club of the Badu House is a favorite place for local performers to gather and share their talents. To encourage more participants and larger audiences, the Badu House hosted Llano's first Amateur Night on January 26, 1984. Since Sam also prides himself on being a great chili chef, what more appropriate dish to serve for everyone who wanted to "ham it up and jam it up"? Here is Sam's genuine Texas red chili recipe, along with his comments. You know how these lawyers are, anxious to impress you with their knowledge.

3 pounds lean beef or venison, coarsely ground
⅛ pound suet
3 ounces tomato paste
18 ounces Texas-brewed beer
1 medium onion, finely chopped
1 tablespoon freshly ground oregano leaves
1½ tablespoons freshly ground cumin (comino) seeds
⅛ teaspoon finely ground pequins (if fresh, 3 crushed)
1½ tablespoons black pepper
3 medium cloves garlic, crushed
2 tablespoons salt
9 mild, dark red chili pods (fresh if available, dehydrated acceptable)
1 tablespoon masa harina

In a large skillet, put meat with ⅛ pound suet or sufficient cooking oil to braise the meat. After braising, put meat in large pot and add tomato paste, beer, and chopped onion. Add just enough water to cover the mixture and simmer for a few minutes. Grind oregano, cumin, pequins, and pepper in perfectly dry blender if a hand grinder and *metate* are not available. Add to meat with crushed garlic and salt. Stir thoroughly and remove from heat.

Boil chili pods until soft in as little water as possible, then remove seeds and stems. Place pods and their water in a blender and blend until a liquid sauce. Add chili sauce to the meat and simmer for at least 2 hours. Longer may be necessary if wild game is used. Allow 30 minutes before removing from heat to add the masa harina, which has been well blended with water for thickening. The masa harina adds a delicious Mexican flavor and aroma to the chili. Remember, water can always be added if the chili is too thick.

If you like your chili *muy caliente* (very hot), while chili is simmering flavor it with more dried pequins, fresh pequins, ground cayenne pepper, or Tabasco sauce.

Sam's favorite chilies are the long red Anaheims, fresh or dehydrated. But they are not always available, and a good grade fresh chili powder is certainly suitable with a 1-tablespoon-per-pod conversion. Beware of commercial powders with various other seasonings. Use plain chili powder *without* the oregano, etc.

Sam advises that even though there are many, many recipes for making chili, the importance lies in the order in which certain items are blended and in which spices are added. His is the method that brings out the best flavor in the spices.

(Note: The amateur night was such an overwhelming success that patrons wanted one held every week. Heaven forbid! The Badu House agreed to four times a year.)

Texas Chocolate Pecan Cake

2 cups flour
2 cups sugar
2 sticks margarine
4 tablespoons cocoa
1 cup water
2 eggs
1 teaspoon baking soda
1 teaspoon vanilla
½ cup buttermilk

Combine flour and sugar in mixing bowl. Melt magarine with cocoa and water, and pour over flour and sugar mixture. Mix above together well, stirring by hand. Add eggs, baking soda, vanilla, and buttermilk. Mix well again by hand. Pour in greased 13½ x 9½-inch pan. Bake at 350° for 25 to 30 minutes.

Topping
1 stick butter or magarine
4 tablespoons cocoa
½ cup milk
½ cup chopped pecans
1 16-ounce box confectioners' sugar

Soften butter in a small saucepan. Add cocoa and milk, and bring to a boil. Pour over confectioners' sugar and stir well. Add nuts and pour over cake.

Hotel
Blessing
Blessing

Blessing

Blessing, Texas, established in 1880, went twenty-three years without a name. So when founder Jonathan Pierce decided to name it "Thank God," residents felt it was really a blessing. But the postal service officials had different ideas and rejected the Pierce petition. He was still determined, however, to thank God for the two railroads that had finally reached them. As a result, Pierce chose the name of Blessing, for it surely was a blessing when progress finally arrived at the little train stop. To commemorate this occasion, Pierce then built Hotel Blessing, a godsend indeed to those in need of a hearty meal, a hot cup of coffee, and heartwarming hospitality.

Blessing had its beginnings long before it was christened. It began when Jonathan came to Texas from Rhode Island to meet his brother, the famous Texas cattleman Abel Head (Shanghai) Pierce. Both were apparently able-headed, as both made Texas-sized fortunes. The 1904 Hotel Blessing, once the place to stay for real-estate promoters and ranchers, was one result of this family fortune.

And in the family the old hotel stayed until the Pierces decided to donate it to the Blessing Historical Society. At present, the society is in the process of restoring it. The gray and white mission-style building houses twenty-five guest rooms, all sparsely furnished for the time being with old (not antique) furniture. In fact, if you are looking to make a donation to a worthy cause, the Hotel Blessing is your chance. The historical society encourages any interested visitor to air-condition a room, donate a painting of a Blessing forefather, or pave a parking space, to name a few ideas. Rooms are presently cooled by Texas breezes, aided by ceiling fans. None has a private bath, but rates are very reasonable to compensate.

Also reasonable is the down-home–style food. Served in the no-frills restaurant with its long wooden tables, red and white plastic tablecloths, and exposed plumbing, the food is some of the best in the Lone Star state. Breakfast is served at 6 A.M. You can choose from steak, sausage, ham, bacon, hotcakes, eggs, grits, and toast. Coffee is "serve-your-own" and "cast your coin in the can." At lunch, the buffet-style fare is plentiful, with diners serving themselves from huge cast-iron pots kept warm on old gas-converted wood stoves. Until recently guests went freely in and out of the kitchen to help themselves. To improve the flow of traffic, however, the stoves were moved into the dining room. And so much is served that you can't possibly eat it all. There is a choice of barbeque, fried chicken, beef tips, fried Gulf fish, chicken-fried steak, and vegetables in abundance, such as green beans, rice, pinto beans, collard greens, mashed potatoes and cream gravy, and squash.

As for the camaraderie, take time to visit with the regular cowboy crowd. You'll recognize them because they always sit at the corner table, their customary spot. So, partner, bring along a Texas-sized appetite, a Texas-sized heart, and a donation or two when you visit Hotel Blessing. Manager Helen Feldhousen and her helpers are certainly generous with all of us by providing endless fare for a mere four bucks.

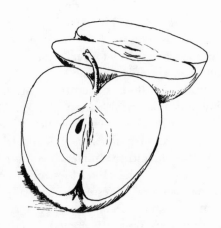

Helen Feldhousen's Chocolate Pie

Yields 1 8-inch or 9-inch pie

People have been coming to the Blessing Coffee Shop for a lot of years. The rooms may have been closed, but Helen Feldhousen was in the kitchen creating legends in food. Back in the old days, you just went in the kitchen with your plate, helped yourself to whatever was simmering on the stove, sat down at your table, and ate until you could hardly move. The stoves are still serving mountains of food, but they have been moved into the dining room, and the kitchen is off limits. Regardless, a meal at the Blessing is always memorable.

1 cup sugar
¼ cup flour
5 tablespoons cocoa
2 cups milk
3 egg yolks
1 teaspoon vanilla
1 tablespoon butter
1 baked 8-inch or 9-inch pie shell

Sift sugar, flour, and cocoa together. Add 1 cup of milk and mix. Then mix egg yolks in the other cup of milk and beat. Add egg and milk mixture to the first mixture. Cook in a double boiler until thick. Add vanilla and butter. Stir and pour into pie shell. Cool and put meringue on top.

Meringue
3 egg whites
7 tablespoons sugar

Beat egg whites until stiff. Add sugar gradually. Spread over pie. Brown in 350° oven for 12 minutes.

White Bread

Yields 4 loaves

4 ¼ cups warm water
¼ cup sugar
3 tablespoons shortening
5 teaspoons salt
3 packages yeast
12 cups flour

Put warm water in large bowl. Add sugar, shortening, salt, and yeast. Let sit 10 minutes. Add 4 cups flour and mix thoroughly. Add remaining flour gradually and mix to a dough that won't stick to hands. Knead 8 to 10 minutes. Placed in greased bowl and let rise in warm place until doubled in bulk. Knead down and make 4 loaves. Place in greased pans. Let rise again until doubled in bulk. Bake in 350° oven for 45 minutes.

Driskill
Hotel
Austin

Even older than the present Capitol building, the Driskill Hotel has seen a lot of politicians vie for office not only in Texas, but also in Washington, D.C. If the walls of this historic hotel could talk, they would probably tell us of a mind-boggling range and scope of private agreements that have been concluded here among governors, senators, representatives, lobbyists, appointees, and bureaucrats. Since 1886, if there were such a thing as the state hotel of Texas, it would have to have been the Driskill.

Jesse Lincoln Driskill was quite an entrepreneur, and during the Civil War he made his fortune selling beef to a starving Confederacy. When the big cattle drives began, Colonel Driskill was one of the first Texans to "head 'em up and roll 'em out" across the mighty Red River for those hungry Yankee markets.

When the Colonel arrived in Austin, he decided a great capital needed a great hotel. Driskill's decision resulted in a Romanesque structure that looked completely out of place on Austin's muddy 6th Street (Pecan Street, in those days). But the Driskill set the tone for this frontier capital. Electric lights glowed for the first time west of St. Louis at the hotel, and Austin's first telegrams arrived at the Driskill. Even the first long distance telephone call was from the Driskill to Wichita, Kansas. Such progressive features were protected by the hotel's own fire department, also the first in Austin.

The historic landmark has undergone some traumatic renovations during its years. The original entrance became a deserted hall of massive pillars, and the bar changed decor so often that no version was memorable. The unimportant guest rated a tiny cubbyhole room lost somewhere in a maze of hallways.

Fortunately, grand dames have a way of enduring and rising above their misfortunes. Future plans call for rooms furnished in antiques, the original entrance to be used again, and the reception desk moved.

The LBJ Suite will still offer its elegant accoutrements, and the bungalow on the roof will still bill itself as "The Best Little Penthouse in Texas." Also, the gorgeous gold-leaf mirrors in the Maximilian Rooms that were Emperor Maximilian's gift to the beautiful Carlota will still reflect the crystal chandeliers and dark red tapestries of the ballroom.

Continuing to maintain its best traditions, the Driskill Dining Room remains one of the best quietly elegant restaurants in Austin.

Spicy Shortribs

Serves 6

5 pounds shortribs, cut in 2-inch pieces
5 cups canned tomatoes
2 cups water
¼ cup chopped onion
1 tablespoon horseradish
1 teaspoon salt
Dash pepper
Dash ground ginger
1½ bay leaves

Brown shortribs. Drain excess fat. Mix rest of ingredients and pour over ribs. Cover and bake at 350° for 1 hour.

Seafood Gumbo

Serves 55

Yes, this recipe makes 55 delicious savory cups of rich seafood gumbo. When you are one of the best restaurants in Austin, however, 55 cups may not be enough.

- 3 pounds onions, diced
- 3 pounds celery, diced
- 2 pounds bell peppers, chopped
- 8 cloves garlic
- 3 tablespoons basil leaves
- 3 tablespoons ground oregano
- 2 tablespoons thyme
- 5 bay leaves
- 2 cups gumbo filé
- 5 pounds shrimp, peeled and deveined
- 5 pounds scallops
- 1 No. 10 can (12½ cups) whole tomatoes, crushed
- 1½ gallons water
- 5 cups cooked rice
- Tabasco sauce

Sauté onion, celery, and bell peppers. Add spices, shrimp, and scallops. Cook 4 to 5 minutes. Add tomatoes and water. Bring to a rapid boil and thicken with butter roux. Remove from heat and add rice. Stir well. Season with Tabasco sauce.

Roux
1½ cups butter
1½ cups flour

Melt butter in heavy skillet over medium heat. Stir in flour gradually. Lower heat. It is very important that you keep *stirring constantly*. After the flour has been combined with the butter, turn heat down very low and cook until golden brown, *stirring constantly*.

Excelsior House
Jefferson

The Excelsior House has withstood it all — the Reconstruction era, the wrath of railroad magnate Jay Gould, and the subsequent absence of the Texas Pacific Railway Company and the decline of the steamboat. Never once has it closed its doors, though its very existence was threatened by a demolition crew in 1961. Thanks to a group of dedicated historians — the Jessie Allen Wise Garden Club, who purchased the hotel for $30,000 — it is now considered one of the most beautiful historic hotels in Texas.

The mid-nineteenth-century hotel, built by a New Hampshire sea captain named Perry, was first christened the Irvine House. No one knows when or why the name was changed to the Excelsior House, except that early brochures quote a passage from Longfellow's "Excelsior":

> A traveller, by the faithful hound,
> Half-buried in the snow was found,
> Still grasping in his hand of ice
> That banner with the strange device.
> Excelsior!

The hotel is indeed a "reach above," with its owners constantly striving ever upward to preserve the showcase that it is. In fact, the 1961 restoration spurred a historical revival in Jefferson that has resulted in the city's acquiring for its historic landmarks fifty Texas Historic Medallions. The garden club has furnished the New Orleans–style structure with period antiques, some bequeathed to the Excelsior by Jefferson residents, though many of the pieces are original to the hotel. The beautiful Oriental rugs, ornate chandeliers, and Victorian wallpaper add grace and elegance to every unique room, so that you feel you are in a home rather than a hotel.

The rooms are all quite lovely, though I would recommend asking for one of the showrooms (the garden club gives tours daily) if you plan to stay overnight. Each is decorated with a particular theme and person in mind. For instance, the Presidential Suite is spectacular with rich

31

red wallpaper, a sumptuous bathroom, and a magnificent four-poster bed with a ten-foot canopy. The Sleigh Room is furnished with a sleigh (yes, a sleigh) bed and matching dresser. (A third piece, a chest of drawers, is found elsewhere in the hotel.) This set of sleigh furniture is one of only three in existence. If you are a Lady Bird fan, you might want to stay in the Lady Bird Johnson Room, decorated with some of the hotel's original rosewood furniture. There is also a clock in this room that Lady Bird's father gave to his bride as a wedding present. When visiting her hometown in nearby Karnack, Mrs. Johnson always occupies this room.

To commemorate the most sensational trial in Jefferson's history, there is also the Diamond Bessie Room (see related story, The Magnolias). Bessie Moore and her new husband, Abe Rothschild, stayed at the Excelsior in 1877, and it was during this stay that Bessie was murdered. They left their room one Sunday for a picnic by the Big Cypress. Bessie did not return with her husband, who was sporting Bessie's diamonds. Her body was later discovered, and after seven years of trials, Abe was found innocent. Some say he bribed jurors with $1,000 each. At any rate, their picture hangs in this room.

Railroad boss Jay Gould has also been immortalized by the Excelsior House's addition of the Jay Gould Room. Actually, it would be incorrect to assume that Gould was a town hero, since he was instrumental in calling a halt to Jefferson's prosperity. Gould came to the town in 1872 for the purpose of acquiring the right-of-way for his railroad. City fathers wanted the businessman to purchase land from them, but he refused. He was so angered by the failure of the deal that he signed the Excelsior guest register with "End of Jefferson, Jan. 2, 1872." He also walked the bill in protest. Some say Gould ensured his curse would come true by blowing up the dam, which resulted in the Big Cypress's becoming unnavigable. In the 1870s, before this event, Jefferson accommodated 38,000 residents, more people than any city in Texas. A steamboat port for riverboats traveling from Jefferson to New Orleans, it was known as "the Gateway of Texas" and "Queen of the Cypress." As a result of the decline in steamboat trade, Jefferson's economy began to falter. Whether Gould had anything to do with the incident remains to be proved. However, Gould must still be angry, as some believe his ghost resides in his namesake room. One maid refuses to go inside, and even Steven Spielberg, director of *E. T.* and *Poltergeist,* who stayed in the room, left it at 2 A.M. one morning complaining of strange occurrences.

Whether you stay in the Jay Gould Room, the Presidential Suite, or a comfortable unnamed room, be sure to enjoy the only meal served at the Excelsior House, a plantation breakfast of ham, eggs, grits, and the famous Orange-Blossom Muffins. The coffee is Louisiana chicory, a brew that will keep you awake for days. Breakfast is served in the sunny solarium that overlooks the courtyard. Be sure to notice the twenty-place mahogany table in the dining room, along with the beautiful concert grand piano. What more could one want but to start the day sipping coffee and having one of the Excelsior House's famous Orange-Blossom Muffins?

Orange-Blossom Muffins

Makes 1 dozen

The plantation breakfast at the Excelsior House became a Texas tradition when the first Orange-Blossom Muffins became part of the menu. The late manager, Cissy McCampbell, introduced this marvelous treat many years ago when the Excelsior House was the only operating historic inn in Texas. Not only was your room a treasured memory, but breakfast in the patio room or in the formal dining room became one of life's special moments. Thick slices of ham, bacon, or sausage, along with fresh eggs, good old southern grits, and aromatic coffee were all wonderful, but the main attraction was a basket of those muffins with their special orange flavor.

The Excelsior House has continued its standards of excellence through the years, and the plantation breakfast has remained unchanged. This recipe for the fabled Orange-Blossom Muffins can be found in many cookbooks; you have not truly experienced the Excelsior House until you savor this famous recipe.

1 slightly beaten egg
¼ cup sugar
½ cup orange juice (fresh or frozen)
2 tablespoons salad oil
2 cups packaged biscuit mix
½ cup orange marmalade
½ cup ground pecans

Combine first four ingredients. Add biscuit mix and beat vigorously for 30 seconds. Stir in marmalade and pecans. Grease muffin pans or line with paper baking cups; fill two-thirds full.

Topping
¼ cup sugar
1½ tablespoons all-purpose flour
½ teaspoon cinnamon
¼ teaspoon nutmeg
1 tablespoon butter or margarine

Combine sugar, flour, cinnamon, and nutmeg. Cut in butter until crumbly. Sprinkle over batter in muffin tins. Bake at 400° for 20 to 25 minutes.

Yellow Squash Casserole

Serves 6

In keeping with the Old South flavor of Jefferson and the Excelsior House, this real southern dish is often prepared for special occasions.

3 pounds yellow squash
1 large onion, chopped
2 tablespoons butter
1 egg, beaten
⅛ pound Velveeta cheese
1 tablespoon seasoned salt
Dash salt
Dash cayenne pepper
½ cup crumbled cracker crumbs
Butter for topping

Wash, cut up, and cook squash in salted water. When tender, drain water and mash squash. Sauté chopped onion in 2 tablespoons butter and add to squash. Add beaten egg to mixture. Chip half the cheese into squash. Add seasoned salt, salt, and cayenne pepper. Place in ungreased casserole. Sprinkle cracker crumbs on top and dot with rest of cheese and butter. Cook at 350° for 1 hour.

Tortoni Squares

Serves 9

Special parties are held at the Excelsior House, and its kitchen turns out marvelous treats for luncheons and receptions. This easy dessert is so delicious it will bring a gourmet flair to any repast.

1⅓ cups vanilla wafers, finely crushed
⅓ cup toasted almonds, chopped
1 teaspoon almond extract
3 tablespoons melted butter or margarine
3 pints vanilla ice cream, softened
1 12-ounce jar apricot preserves
Whipped cream

Mix vanilla wafer crumbs, almonds, extract, and butter. Butter a 9-inch square pan. Layer crumbs on the bottom of the pan, then ice cream, and then apricot preserves. Sprinkle with crumbs. Repeat layers, ending with crumbs on top. Freeze several hours until ice cream is firm. Cut in squares and top with whipped cream.

Farris
1912
Eagle Lake

Thousands of ducks and geese and flocks of hunters, photographers, and bird-watchers find their way each winter to Eagle Lake. What makes this area so popular? For the birds, it's the ideal upper Texas coast tall-grass prairie, and for the hunters and nature lovers, it's the Farris 1912. Known as the "goose-hunting capital of the world," Eagle Lake is the epitome of a sportsman's paradise, with light and dark Canadian and white-fronted (specklebelly) geese, thirteen species of ducks including wood ducks and mallards, and plenty of freshwater fish lying in wait for the angler's lure. And amid all this nature, the restored Farris 1912 provides a dry, gracious place to lay one's head and taste great food that is "a little bit country" and "a little bit class."

The hotel, resurrected in 1977 by proprietors Bill and Helyn Farris, sits on the town square site that has been the spot of a hotel since 1857, the year of Eagle Lake's birth. It was in that first year that the Good Hotel was built as an old stagecoach stop. It provided the tired drummer with a bed, one chair, and a nail to hang his hat on. A tin basin on an old wooden soapbox was used to wash off the train dust. In 1912 the old building was replaced by a brand-new structure called Hotel Dallas. Designed by A. E. Baines (also architect for the stately homes on Houston's Courtland Place and the Link-Lee Mansion, which is now the administration building of the University of St. Thomas), the hotel was known as "the finest small-town hotel in the state." It was considered an uptown railway hotel, since it had indoor plumbing, hot and cold water, multiple skylights, velvet draperies, and chandeliers. Later called the Hotel Ramsey, it went into decline and finally closed as a result of the failing railroad industry and the rise of the auto and motel industries.

Bill and Helyn Farris came to its rescue in 1974. After four years of hard work, the hotel was rechristened the Farris 1912, in keeping with the tradition created by the Good and Dallas hotels. As a result, the new hotel carries the name of its owner and the year 1912 to commemorate Eagle Lake's golden era.

The beautifully restored old red brick building houses twenty-four rooms of high-quality antiques, including old chandeliers, lamps, and ceiling fans. There is the Drummer's Room, where good food is served; a solarium, perfect for parties and receptions; and a comfortable mezzanine. Just off the solarium is a well-stocked floral and gift shop. There are sixteen bedrooms, two of which have private baths, while others share baths. There are lavatories in all the brightly painted guest rooms (one is purple), which are furnished with period wardrobes and iron beds. Some are even furnished with wicker. If this isn't large enough for your hunting party, the Guest House, the sister building to the Farris, is also available. It was built in the 1920s, and the furnishings are more modern than those found in the main building. The rooms are rented as four suites with a bedroom, a sitting room that doubles as a second bedroom, and a bath.

In the main building, breakfast is provided when you rent a room. For guests who come during the hunting-season months of November, December, and January, the Farris 1912 offers the American Plan. Three "all you can eat" gourmet meals are provided, including a 4:30 A.M. country breakfast. Bill and Helyn also serve hors d'oeuvres before dinner, in addition to snacks and setups. When you leave in the morning, your thermos will be filled with coffee or hot chocolate, and when you return, your dry shoes will be waiting for you in the "mud shed" on the parking lot. The Farris will also provide transportation to the hotel from the airport. Be sure to call Helyn to get details on when the main building is open. It closes in the summer, but the Guest House is open all year.

If you're a bird-watcher, you'll be interested in knowing that the Attwater Prairie Chicken National Wildlife Refuge, a 798-acre refuge of native prairies, croplands, ponds, and woodlands, is only six miles from Eagle Lake. Since 1973, 250 species of birds have been recorded, including 200 of 1,500 remaining Attwater's prairie chickens, a species that once numbered more than one million in Texas.

The recipes here are compliments of Helyn Farris. Note that among them is the wild game dish Quail with White Grapes, a delicious entrée served in the hotel restaurant and one so reminiscent of the hunting grounds of Eagle Lake.

Quail with White Grapes

Serves 6

Since Eagle Lake is a bird hunter's idea of paradise, one of the favorite dishes at the Farris 1912 is Helyn's gourmet quail. However, the Farris favorite is not in the least complicated.

12 quail
6 tablespoons melted butter
4 cups dry white wine
2 cups seedless white grapes, cut in half lengthwise
¾ cup blanched almonds, sliced
8 tablespoons flour
Salt and pepper to taste
Kitchen Bouquet

Place quail in roasting pan. Brush with melted butter, and pour wine over birds. Bake at 350° about 45 minutes. Add grapes and almonds. Baste birds with sauce in pan and cook 10 minutes longer or until done. Remove quail from pan. Keep warm. Add flour to pan drippings and whisk until the consistency of gravy. Add salt and pepper to taste and a few drops of Kitchen Bouquet for color. Serve quail with grape and almond gravy poured over them. Delicious with wild rice.

Japanese Fruit Pie

Yields 1 8-inch pie

1 stick margarine, melted
2 eggs, well beaten
½ cup raisins
1 cup pecans, chopped
1 cup flaked coconut
1 cup sugar
1 tablespoon white vinegar
1 8-inch unbaked pie shell

Melt margarine and let cool. Add remaining ingredients. Mix well. Pour into pie shell. Bake at 325° for 40 minutes.
Delicious with ice cream and served warm.

Roquefort or Blue Cheese Dressing

Yields 2½ cups

During hunting season, when Helyn and Bill have a lot of hungry hunters to feed, snacks are served in the upstairs lobby to enhance all those tales about "the one that got away." Here is Helyn's dip for raw vegetables, which also makes a great salad dressing.

1 cup sour cream
1 cup mayonnaise (Do not substitute. This *must* be mayonnaise.)
1 2-ounce package of Roquefort or blue cheese
Juice of ½ lemon
1 clove garlic or ½ teaspoon garlic powder (do not use garlic salt)

Mix all ingredients in a blender or mixer until smooth. Let the dressing ripen in the refrigerator overnight.

Ozark Pudding

Serves 4

1 egg
¾ cup sugar
2 tablespoons flour
¼ teaspoon baking powder
⅛ teaspoon salt
½ cup pecans, chopped
½ cup apples, finely chopped with skins
1 teaspoon vanilla
2 tablespoons flour

Beat egg and sugar until smooth. Combine flour, baking powder, and salt. Stir into egg mixture. Add nuts, apples, and vanilla. Bake in a heavily buttered pie pan in 350° oven for 35 minutes.

Best when served warm with a big dollop of whipped cream.

The Faust
New Braunfels

When the Faust opened its doors in 1928, it was alive with the sights and sounds of the Roaring Twenties. Even though the hotel bore the unglamorous name of the Travelers Inn, people came here to enjoy the German town of New Braunfels. During World War II, San Antonio–based soldiers and their brides began honeymooning here so often that the hotel was renamed the Honeymoon Hotel.

In the 1950s the honeymoon was over for the hotel, and it went into bankruptcy. Taken over by a local bank, this three-story yellow brick lodging establishment was christened the Faust after the bank's president. The Krueger family owned the Faust before its renovation. (Bob Krueger was Ambassador to Mexico under President Carter.)

An extensive restoration was done later, and this old hotel is now absolutely charming. Much of the structure and decoration is original, including the beautifully intricate red tile floor in the lobby, the numerous ceiling fans, wrought-iron light fixtures, and the old cash register still used at the front desk. Some of the porcelain bath fixtures and the few remaining claw-foot tubs are also original.

Rooms are fairly small, but that is the way they were back in the 1920s. To compensate, many have original pieces of furniture that add to the nostalgia of the Faust. All are air-conditioned, with television and a funky candlestick telephone. Even though the Faust is proud of its romantic atmosphere, it also wants to please the commercial trade.

The Veranda Restaurant provides a very pleasant setting in which to enjoy your Veal Faust or any other of their delectable menu items. Plants, bentwood furniture, and period accessories such as "tombstone" radios add to the charm. Be sure to enjoy a drink in the lounge with its beautiful handmade teak and mahogany bar.

The following recipes are compliments of Faust Chef Ervin Carter, who was gracious enough to share his favorites.

Veal Faust

Serves 8

2 eggs
2 cups milk
2 cups fine cracker meal
Salt
Pepper
8 veal slices
8 slices mozzarella cheese
8 cherry tomatoes
24 avocado slices

Mix eggs and milk for egg wash. Mix cracker meal, salt, and pepper. Dip veal cutlet into egg wash; bread with cracker-meal mixture. Fry in small frying pan until brown; turn. Veal cutlet should be golden brown. Place veal cutlet on dinner plate. Put one slice of mozzarella cheese on cutlet, one cherry tomato on cheese, three slices of avocado around tomato. Place plate in warm oven until cheese melts. Serve hot.

German Sauerkraut

Serves 8

If you think of sauerkraut as shredded cabbage soaked in brine, you are absolutely correct. The Faust's sauerkraut recipe is more on the order of boiled cabbage, but it is a delicious way to serve Germany's favorite vegetable.

¼ pound bacon
2 medium onions, chopped
2 apples, unpeeled and sliced
1 medium raw potato, chopped
2 pounds cabbage, shredded
½ cup water
1 teaspoon salt
½ cup sugar

Sauté bacon, onions, apples, and potato until tender. Add cabbage, water, salt, and sugar. Cover and cook until cabbage is tender, approximately 35 to 45 minutes.

Gruene Mansion
Gruene

Forget the "u" when you pronounce this town with the German name of Gruene. It is just plain old "Grene." This tiny hamlet is a prime example of how well nostalgia sells these days. From a ragtag smattering of decrepit old buildings, Gruene is now one of the most popular tourist spots in the Hill Country.

Nearly every building in this family-owned town was constructed by a German immigrant, H. D. Gruene. Cotton was king in Gruene, so in 1878 a cotton gin became a necessity. H. D. also built his mercantile building and several houses. Still standing is the 1850s house occupied by Ernst Gruene, H. D.'s father.

H. D. was the typical hardworking German, but he also knew that there was more to life in those pioneer days than picking cotton. This benevolent landlord also built a dance hall and saloon to provide entertainment for his family and tenants.

The 1920s brought disaster to Gruene's town. H. D. died in 1920, and a few years later the boll weevil and Depression arrived to hasten the town's death. However, like the phoenix from the ashes, Gruene has risen again. The burned ruins of the first cotton gin now house a popular restaurant, the Grist Mill. The "new" electric gin constructed in 1922 is a restaurant and also one of Texas's first commercial experiments in wines, the Guadalupe Valley Winery. Gruene Hall positively bursts at the seams with dancers intent on mastering the Cotton-Eyed Joe and Texas Two-Step. Gift shops, toy makers, and potters add to the atmosphere.

To really soak up the true spirit of Gruene, why not rent a Victorian mansion in the heart of "downtown"? Wraparound porches topped with a gingerbread cupola enclose four bedrooms and three baths with everything furnished. All you have to supply is your food, if you want to cook, and your toothbrush. Five acres of Guadalupe River property also include several outbuildings with accommodations. Who can resist staying in River Barn I or River Barn II? If a barn is not your idea of a weekend, how about the Corn Crib? You don't have to bring your own hay, either. The furnishings are just as super as in the Mansion.

Gruene Apple Pecan Bread

Yields 1 loaf

Preheat oven to 350° and be sure all ingredients are at room temperature.

      1½ cups sifted all-purpose flour
      ½ teaspoon salt
      1 teaspoon baking soda
      1½ cups whole-grain flour
      ¼ cup shortening
      ½ cup sugar
      1 egg
      ¾ cup apple, grated
      ¼ cup apple juice
      1 cup buttermilk
      1 cup pecan pieces

Sift together all-purpose flour, salt, and baking soda. Add whole-grain flour. Cream shortening and sugar in a large bowl. Beat in egg. Add grated apple and apple juice. Mix dry ingredients with the fruit mixture. Add buttermilk, a little at a time. Fold in pecan pieces. Place dough in greased loaf pan. Bake about 1½ hours. Let bread cool in pan before removing.

Chicken Marinade for Grilled or Fried Chicken

2 cups water
1½ cups white wine
¼ large package or 1 small package Good Seasons Italian Dressing
(mix according to directions on back using apple cider vinegar)

Mix all ingredients in 5-gallon container and marinate chicken for at least 24 hours. This makes enough to marinate 15 chicken breasts.

For grilled chicken, cook on grill. Then pour marinade over chicken and serve with lemon-butter sauce.

For fried chicken, cover both sides with flour and deep fry for about 8 minutes. Top with marinade and serve with cream gravy.

Noodles with Spinach and Mushrooms

Serves 4 to 6

1 clove garlic, minced fine
1 pound mushrooms, washed and sliced thick
½ stick butter
½ pound spinach, washed, stemmed, coarsely chopped
½ pint heavy cream
Grated Parmesan cheese
Salt and white pepper
4 cups cooked flat noodles

Sauté garlic and mushrooms in butter. When mushrooms are tender, add the spinach and cook 3 or 4 minutes. Stir in cream and reduce for 2 to 3 minutes. Thicken with grated cheese to desired taste and consistency. Season with salt and white pepper. Pour over hot noodles and serve immediately.

This is wonderful!

Gunter
Hotel
San Antonio

Jot Gunter, a Civil War veteran who served with Dick Dowling, was a lawyer and entrepreneur who knew a shrewd deal when it came his way. Not many people know where Gunter, Texas, is, which was also named for Jot. But the Gunter Hotel is world-famous. Even the site of the Gunter is historic. Back in the days when the Vance Brothers ran a stage line, they opened an inn. In 1857 it became an army barracks, and Robert E. Lee slept here. At the start of the Civil War, United States troops in Texas surrendered to the Confederacy in these barracks.

After the Civil War, the old barracks became a hotel again but were torn down to make room for the first steel building in San Antonio, the Gunter Hotel. Another hotel was under construction in 1907, and there was a fierce race to see which would open first. The Gunter won over the St. Anthony.

Back in its heyday, the Gunter was *the* hotel for Texas cattlemen wearing their traditional sober black suits set off with immaculate white shirts. The glittering stars of the entertainment world might have stayed at the glamorous St. Anthony, but the big cattle deals were made at the Gunter. In 1925 the Gunter received three more stories and the world's first hotel coffee shop. It seemed destined for great things.

Sadly, the hotel did not escape the fate of so many downtown hotels, and it became shabbier and shabbier. Tacky mirrors lined the lobby walls, garish red appeared everywhere, and linoleum covered the floors. Most depressing of all were the seedy rooms; it appeared that the poor old Gunter was irretrievably on the skids. Fortunately, a masterpiece of restoration has once again placed the Gunter in the upper echelon of luxury hotels.

Today when you enter this historic hotel, its quiet elegance is very impressive, particularly if you saw the lobby in the early 1980s. The ornate ceiling, frieze, and old brass mail chute are about the only decorations left from the original lobby. While everything else is brand new, it is all in such good taste that you feel the Gunter really did look this way in its great past.

In the Padre Muldoon Bar, a fantastically handsome brass rail with noble lions' heads frames the bar. Stained-glass windows abound, and a great rotating spit of paddle fans stirs the air. Overstuffed chairs, shelves lined with books, and paneled walls create intimate nooks for a cozy rendezvous. Padre Muldoon was the Catholic priest supplied to the colonists of Stephen F. Austin when Mexico insisted that all Anglos become Catholics. Muldoon was known more for his humor and delightful stories, particularly after numerous swigs on a handy jug, than he was for his zeal in making converts. If the Padre Muldoon stories are true, the good father would absolutely love this bar named in his honor.

One of the important factors in the decision to renovate and save the Gunter was the restoration of the gorgeous Majestic Theatre just across the street. The hotel was purchased by a group of Swiss businessmen, and no expense has been spared to create a European ambience. Rooms are spacious, with warm furnishings and all the amenities of a truly first-class hotel. A wonderful glass-enclosed terrace overlooks busy Houston Street and is used for afternoon teas and receptions.

As for dining, the Cafe Swiss is just off the lobby. Dark paneled walls and ceilings add atmosphere to the wingback chairs, starched white linens, and formal place settings. Touches of Art Deco blend in with Swiss bells and antiques. Cafe Swiss caters to the before- and after-theater crowds, with light suppers as well as heavier fare.

In keeping with the hotel's Swiss flavor, the new owners have opened a Swiss pastry shop. You have to have a will of iron to pass up the éclairs, Black Forest cakes, tarts, strudels, croissants, and endless variety of cookies — all positively guaranteed to be loaded with luscious calories.

Steak Tartare

Serves 2

Steak Tartare is *not* raw ground hamburger meat. True Steak Tartare is ground filet of beef, highly seasoned. Nobody really knows how it originated, though many stories are told. The Swiss say it's from their country, yet the Germans and French say they invented it. Former chef Paul Rossmeier, who contributed this recipe, believes it came to Western Europe by way of the Slavic countries when the Tartars invaded Europe. This truly continental dish is becoming very popular in the United States.

1 raw egg yolk
1 ounce cognac
3 anchovy filets, chopped
½ onion, chopped very fine
½ ounce capers, ground
1 sprig parsley, chopped
1 teaspoon Dijon mustard
7 ounces filet of beef, ground
½ ounce cornichons, chopped
Salt and pepper to taste
Dash Worcestershire sauce

Mix egg yolk, cognac, anchovies, onion, capers, parsley, and mustard thoroughly in a small wooden bowl. Add remaining ingredients. Form into a ball and garnish with parsley.

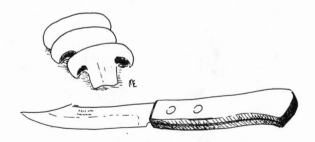

Veal à la Zurich

Serves 4

The cattlemen of the Gunter's past probably never rhapsodized over the pleasures of a really fine piece of veal prepared in a continental style, but the Swiss chefs have mastered the art for many years. The Gunter's chefs uphold the European tradition of a fine veal specialty.

1½ ounces butter
12 ounces milk-fed veal, sliced in ½ x 3 x 4-inch strips
1½ cups fresh mushrooms, sliced
½ ounce flour
8 ounces half-and-half
2 ounces white wine
Salt and pepper to taste
Dash whole thyme
Dash marjoram

Melt butter in sauté pan. Sauté veal until it turns white. Add mushrooms and sauté 2 to 3 minutes more. Add flour and stir well. Make sure flour does not burn. Add half-and-half and wine until thickened. If thinner sauce is desired, add more half-and-half. Season with salt, pepper, thyme, and marjoram to taste.

Note: Chef Rossmeier says this same recipe can be used with pork tenderloins or even turkey, but the meat must be cut into strips like the veal.

Swiss Cheese Fondue

Serves 2

Fondue is the national dish of Switzerland, and the Gunter, with its Swiss touches, could not have contributed a more typical recipe. A custom in Switzerland that would certainly appeal to Texans is that whoever loses his bread in the fondue must buy a round of *Kirschwasser* and kiss the girl next to him. Well, Texans might insist on a round of longnecks instead of the *Kirschwasser,* but they always love to kiss a girl.

1 clove garlic
½ pint mild white wine (preferably Swiss)
.7 ounces Emmentaler cheese
2½ ounces Gruyère cheese
1 ounce cornstarch
1½ ounces *Kirschwasser*
Pinch ground nutmeg
Fresh-ground black pepper
1 loaf day-old French bread, cubed

Note: An earthenware pot reduces the chances of burning the cheese.

Rub out crock with the garlic, then heat white wine in crock. When it begins to boil, add the 2 cheeses. Stir constantly in a figure eight motion. When mixture is melted and smooth, mix cornstarch and *Kirschwasser* and add to the cheese to thicken the fondue. Next, add seasoning. Add salt if desired, but be careful, as the cheese may be salty enough. Dip the cubed bread with a fondue fork, but watch out! That fork gets very hot. *Bon appétit!*

Hempstead Inn
Hempstead

One of my fondest childhood memories was being with all of our large family at Grandma's for Sunday lunch. There were three tables to accommodate everybody, with the adults sitting in the dining room and the kids sharing tables in the kitchen and on the porch. The menu was predictable: fried chicken (grandma had a chicken yard so the chickens were always fresh), mouth-watering roast or duck with rice and gravy, fresh butter beans from the garden, sliced homegrown tomatoes, baked sweet potatoes or Grandma's special hot, buttery biscuits, brewed iced tea, and dark-roast chicory coffee ground that very morning. Starchy but scrumptious. It was boardinghouse reach, and though we kids were all afraid that we wouldn't get enough, there was always food left over.

If you can identify with this story and if you yearn to experience those great days again, visit the Hempstead Inn in Hempstead, Texas. Anne and Ghazi Issa don't even resemble the grandmother of my past, but they surely can cook like her, and the boardinghouse reach for food that never stops coming is alive and well and living in this imposing gray clapboard inn. There are no menus, so there are no decisions to make. The custom there is simple; they serve everything. The help-yourself bowls contain four kinds of meat, which might be fried chicken, ribs, meat loaf, corned beef, or fried fish. Since the Issas don't own a can opener, all the vegetables and fruit are farm-fresh and purchased daily from the town's local farmers' markets. Ten to twelve vegetables and fruits (cabbage, potatoes, tomatoes, watermelon, to name a few) are always served each lunch and dinner. Anne and Ghazi season so well that even the hometown folks would approve. And, of course, Hempstead-grown red- and yellow-meated watermelons (they have put Hempstead on the map) are served when in season. Anne and Ghazi are also known by the locals for their delicious "from-scratch" biscuits and cornbread. So popular is the restaurant that Anne and Ghazi decided to close the eight fully furnished upstairs rooms to give themselves more time for meal service.

If you talk to the Issas, they'll be quick to tell you that the inn is their dream come true. Both had been searching for some time for a place they could call home yet house a restaurant. Ghazi, a Lebanese native who has lived most of his life in the United States, and Anne, a native Houstonian, were passing through Hempstead when they saw the For Sale sign in front of the old, decrepit 1915 Parks Hotel, just off U.S. Highway 290. By that afternoon, they owned the hotel without ever having gone inside. The Issas, intrigued with their new purchase, renamed it the Hempstead Inn and began most of the repairs themselves. They learned that the hotel had once served railway passengers who were traveling through Hempstead, known then as "Six-Shooter Junction." The town was given this nickname by rowdy residents who loved to pass the time by shooting out windows and sometimes at the frightened passengers of passing trains. But age took its toll on the Parks Hotel, and on an unknown date it closed. Thanks to Anne and Ghazi, the old hotel is open again, providing food and drink once again to weary travelers and hungry locals.

For a memorable dining experience reminiscent of "the good ole days," look for the signpost with an old-fashioned girl sitting on a quarter moon just off Highway 290. Designed by Anne, the girl on the moon symbolizes her belief that "you have your dreams and you shoot for them." Anne says she shot for the moon herself, and now she's sitting on it.

Helpful Hints from the Hempstead Inn

You might not expect someone with a name like Ghazi Issa to be a great southern-style chef. Ghazi sounds like he would be more at home with moussaka or stuffed grape leaves. But if you want a dining challenge, pull into the Hempstead Inn, loosen your belt, and see if you can eat a full serving of each down-home dish that comes to your plate: black-eyed peas, cabbage, mashed potatoes and gravy, string beans, chicken-fried steak, fried chicken, fried okra, sausage, meat loaf, sweet potatoes, biscuits, cornbread, and then homemade desserts. But those are just a few of Ghazi's culinary arts for the discerning lover of home cooking. And Ghazi is delighted to offer up some good hints for good old-fashioned dishes.

To cook cabbage, get rid of the choke. Brown bacon and onions, then put in the cabbage. No water should be added, and wait until the cabbage cooks down to season.

Always soak chicken in buttermilk. Fry 15 minutes on each side, bone down. Fry big pieces first, then the legs and wings.

For rice and spaghetti, always wait for the water to boil, and add salt and butter before the spaghetti.

Use black pepper only on beef, and white pepper on everything else.

After black-eyed peas come to a boil, turn them off 1 hour, then start to cook again until done.

High Cotton Inn
Bellville

In 1906 merchant Charles W. Hellmuth built a stately Victorian homestead in Bellville for his wife, Emma Anna, and their eight children. That was more than seventy years ago, and the Hellmuth family has been long gone from the 4,000-square-foot house, which is now the High Cotton Inn. Evidence of their love of family and the good life remain, however, for the very structure, with its large accommodating rooms and balconies, giant windows, and open transoms, pulsates warmth and hospitality. Though the new owners, George and Anna Horton, have added bathrooms upstairs, a sitting/television room, a bedroom downstairs, and a back porch that looks out on the pool, the original cypress structure remains intact. Since being extensively renovated, the High Cotton Inn has become Bellville's most impressive attraction. The feeling of space and informality is the answer to the stress-plagued Houston commuter's fondest wishes.

A weekend visitor to this historic bed and breakfast will immediately note that the atmosphere is "laid-back." For example, it is very likely that the Horton pet boxer, Lady, will greet you at your car when you arrive and accompany you as you tour the antique-furnished inn. Anna and George are also unpretentious, and as a result, Bellville neighbors and friends congregate frequently in the High Cotton parlor to swap stories and sing songs.

The student of logic will notice that this wonderful old "B & B" houses a number of anachronisms. The first difference appears as you step through the front door. As a focal point of the formal Victorian facade, you see a rather avant-garde stylized leaded glass door that would not have been accepted by the average turn-of-the-century artisan. The Hortons say that it is original, however, and a comment on Hellmuth's love of design. Anna and George have also added a rather diverse flavor of their own. Though most of the house is furnished with family antiques and decorated with period wallcoverings and accessories, the kitchen, sitting room, and bathrooms are contemporary, adding a somewhat eclectic mood to the inn. In spite of these eccentricities, the High Cotton Inn possesses a historic atmosphere.

The Hortons are quick to note that the inn is eligible for formal Texas historic-structure recognition. They opened the High Cotton in 1983, and there are still plans to convert the roomy attic to house additional guests and to restore the grounds, accented by pecan and fruit trees, to their original state. At present, Anna, George, and their little girl, Campbell, reside downstairs, their quarters composed of the Hellmuth music room, the added bedroom, and an adjoining bath that has a history all its own. This small room was once called the "bride's room" by the Hellmuth family. It was the custom that every one of the five sons bring his new bride to the homestead for a period of one year to learn the art of housekeeping from her mother-in-law.

Guests sleep upstairs in one of the five bedrooms, sharing the two and a half baths and a sitting room that opens up to a veranda. Each room is named after either a relative or a friend of the Hortons, with individual motifs chosen to fit the respective personalities of the namesakes. The Jay Bute Room is named, for example, after the vice-president of Bute Paint Stores in Houston, who donated paint, flooring, and wallpaper for the restoration. The wallpaper, characterized by little ducks, is indicative of Jay's love of duck hunting. Bobby Russell's Room is decorated with the American Indian in mind. Russell, a close friend of the Hortons who donated many weekends to the project, is particularly interested in this subject. In Uncle Buster's Room, named after George's great-uncle Cleveland Sewall, after whom Rice University's Sewall Hall was named, antique buffs will note the Victorian bed that actually belonged to this successful Houstonian. Ella Campbell's Room is decorated in pink, an appropriate color for the feminine Mrs. Campbell. The pitcher and washbasin in this room belonged to Anna's grandmother. The Sallie Sewall Room is named after George's grandmother. Be sure to see Mrs. Sewall's white beaded ball gown displayed in the upstairs parlor. As reigning queen, she wore it to the turn-of-the-century Notsuoh Ball, held every year in Houston from 1899 to 1916 to commemorate the cotton industry. The crocheted tablecloths and lace curtains found throughout the inn were handmade by Marietta Robinson, Anna's mother.

As for the food, Anna's own touch is apparent when she serves her traditional plantation breakfast, which includes eggs, bacon, sausage, homemade pastries and bread, and hot brandied fruit. A bedtime snack is also provided, complete with wine, cheese, fruit, and homemade fudge. Sunday supper is available by reservation. Anna can also handle large groups for brunches and luncheons. The pool on the grounds provides a pleasant setting for a group party. Children are welcomed, though you will have to provide their sleeping bags.

You'll want to soak up some local color while in Bellville, the "Belle of Bluebonnet Country." Though a somewhat sleepy retreat for those accustomed to the bustle of the city, there are a few leisurely diversions. You can fish in the Brazos River; attend local fairs, festivals, and the frequent horse and cattle shows (this is hunter, jumper, quarterhorse, and thoroughbred country); or go horseback riding. You can also visit the Blue Bell Creamery, the Bellville Potato Chip Factory, or spend the day at San Felipe State Park. For dinner, a drive to the Parlour in New Ulm is a must. Once an old funeral parlor, the restaurant and bar not only provides a meeting place for the town's one hundred residents of German ancestry but also is a place to enjoy fresh fried catfish while listening to an oompah quartet. Be sure to ask owner Alton Haverlah to relate his World War I stories. (He was an interpreter while a prisoner in a German prisoner-of-war camp.)

For a weekend away from it all, give the High Cotton Inn a try, and see what it's really like to be "in high cotton."

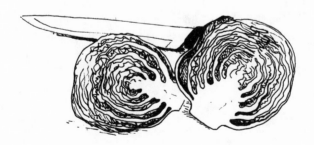

Zucchini Pesto Soup

Serves 6

1 pound zucchini
½ teaspoon salt
1½ cups onions, sliced
3 tablespoons butter or olive oil
2 cups frozen lima beans
1 cup frozen green beans
6 cups boiling water
1 teaspoon salt

Grate zucchini and toss with salt; drain. Cook onions in butter 8 to 10 minutes over low heat. Simmer zucchini with onions until zucchini is tender. Add lima beans, peas, water, and salt. Cook 45 minutes on low heat. Soup may now be refrigerated or served. To serve, bring to simmer, add reserved zucchini juice, and correct seasoning. Ladle into bowls and top with a spoonful of pesto.

Pesto
1 tablespoon pork fat or blanched bacon
2 large cloves garlic
10 to 12 leaves fresh or ½ tablespoon dried basil
3 tablespoons chopped parsley
2 egg yolks
⅓ cup fresh Parmesan cheese, grated
⅓ cup olive oil

Puree pork fat; add garlic. When it becomes a smooth paste, add basil and parsley. Add egg yolks and cheese. Finally, add olive oil. A blender or food processor will give the best results.

Stuffed Mushroom Caps

Serves 6–9

18 large fresh mushrooms
¼ cup butter
6 green onions
1 package frozen spinach soufflé, thawed
Parmesan cheese, grated

Wash and stem mushrooms. Sauté caps in butter just to heat through; drain. In same butter, sauté onions, add thawed spinach soufflé, and cook a few minutes over low heat. Stuff caps with spinach mixture. Arrange in shallow pan. Sprinkle with fresh Parmesan. Broil just enough to heat through. Allow at least 2 per person.

Vassie's Secret Fudge Sauce

Makes 5½ pints

2 pounds unsweetened chocolate
2½ pounds (5 cups) sugar
1 quart whipping cream

Melt chocolate in double boiler over low heat. Dissolve sugar in cream in another double boiler, stirring constantly. Pour melted chocolate into sugar and cream mixture. Continue stirring until thick. Pour into jars and refrigerate. When ready to use, thin with coffee cream. Hardens on ice cream.

Sunday Night Shrimp Creole

Serves 12

½ cup butter
1½ cups green pepper, chopped
1⅓ cups chopped onions
2½ cups celery, diced
½ cup flour
3 29-ounce cans tomatoes
1½ tablespoons salt
Black pepper to taste
2 tablespoons brown sugar
3 bay leaves
8 whole cloves
4 pounds fresh shrimp
2 teaspoons Worcestershire sauce
Tabasco sauce
1 tablespoon lemon juice
¾ cup white wine

Melt butter in 8-quart kettle; add peppers, onions, and celery. Sauté 10 minutes or until vegetables are tender. Remove from heat, add flour, and blend well. Add tomatoes gradually, stirring constantly. Add salt, pepper, brown sugar, bay leaves, and cloves. Bring to boil. Then reduce heat and simmer uncovered over low heat about 45 minutes, stirring occasionally. Clean shrimp while mixture is simmering. Add shrimp to thickened tomato sauce and cook 5 minutes. Add Worcestershire sauce, Tabasco, lemon juice, and wine. Serve over hot rice.

Hyatt Regency
Fort Worth

In the late 1800s and early 1900s, Texas cattlemen and oilmen were worlds apart, each group feeling that the other was misusing the vast lands of their Lone Star state. But time proved the two were not irreconcilable, for they came together to create Fort Worth's Hotel Texas. The hotel was the brainchild of cattle baron, builder, and banker Winfield Scott, who wanted to give a luxury hotel to the city that had made him wealthy. Unfortunately, he died before he could put his plan into action. His dream was not lost, however, for many other prominent cattlemen wanted to show their love for Fort Worth. They had made their fortunes during the great cattle-drive days, when Fort Worth's main street was part of the Chisholm Trail. The city and the pocketbooks of the cattle barons grew, and Fort Worth became the town "where the West begins." And grow it did, spurred on even more by the discovery of oil in Ranger, only eighty miles to the west.

It was then that the oil and cattle barons joined forces to build a hotel. A small group of prominent citizens pooled $1.2 million, and to that sum another $1.8 million was contributed by another eight hundred interested Fort Worth residents. And so Winfield's dream was realized, though the builders decided to honor the state and name it Hotel Texas instead of the Winfield. The "Home of the Cattle Barons" opened in 1921, and Hotel Texas became the social and business center of the city. Everyone who was anybody frequented the swank hotel, and in 1926 Texas celebrated the one-hundredth anniversary of its independence from Mexico there. It was during this event, the Frontier Centennial, that Billy Rose, hired by the hotel to put on an extravaganza, turned down the unknown Weatherford actress Mary Martin for a part. The show was a big success anyway, as were most of the events that took place at the grand Hotel Texas.

That was in its heyday. But the years passed, and the hotel saw many owners and many changes. Finally, in 1979, the Woodbine Development Corporation and Hyatt Hotels Corporation joined forces to create the Hyatt Regency Fort Worth. They completely restored the exterior to its original state with a red brick facade and the terra cotta steer heads that commemorate the cattle industry. The contrast between the exterior and the interior is indeed a lesson in opposites.

The contemporary interior is pure Hyatt Regency, complete with waterfalls, reflecting pools, a glass elevator, and contemporary art, with special emphasis on California art. There is brass and acrylic everywhere, with space and color adding to the overall open feeling and giving the interior a futuristic mood. The teal blues, burgundies, and beiges add a touch of the Texas motif. The rooms are very contemporary and very comfortable, with decor complementing the modern interior rather than the historic exterior of the building. The hotel is now on the National Register of Historic Places.

As for the cuisine, the beautiful Crystal Cactus Restaurant and the Cafe Centennial offer a wide variety of dishes, from continental to nouvelle cuisine. Ed Keeling, the executive chef, specializes in the nouvelle and was associated with Ma Maison in Hollywood and then the Hyatt Corporation for seven years. He has worked alongside the famed Jacques Maximell and has prepared food for such notable figures as Stevie Wonder, Muhammad Ali, Robin Williams, and Dom DeLuise.

Squab with Parsley and Chanterelles

Serves 4

The award for haute cuisine recipes in this cookbook has to go to the Hyatt Regency in Fort Worth. Testing each of the recipes took a lot of time in preparation and in searching for the unusual ingredients. But that is what haute cuisine involves. Just reading these recipes makes you wish you had the time and money to dine on these incredible dishes without having to do the preparation yourself.

All of the Hyatt's recipes were tested except the squab. When a specialty grocery store in Houston was contacted regarding the chanterelles, they said they did carry these exotic yellow mushrooms, and you could purchase them for a mere $22 a pound. People who claim to know their mushrooms testify that you can find chanterelles along Heights Boulevard in Houston. If the alternative is paying $22 a pound, you would expect Heights Boulevard to be jammed with mushroom pickers.

Bone squab. Tear leaves off parsley. Clean chanterelles and cut into quarters. Prepare sauce.

Cook parsley in boiling water for 4 to 5 minutes. Stop the cooking with ice water, dry the leaves, and set aside.

Sauté chanterelles in very hot oil for 1 minute and drain.

Sauté breast and legs of squab with olive oil and butter for 5 minutes. Remove breasts and sauté legs another 5 minutes. Set aside.

Heat parsley with butter and add salt and white pepper to taste.

Sauté chanterelles with butter until they turn a hazelnut color. Add diced shallots.

The Hyatt did not include the price of squab with chanterelles on the recipe, but if you decide you have to try it, we hope your guests will be impressed with your effort and expense.

4 squabs
5 bunches parsley
1 pound chanterelles
Black pepper
2 shallots, diced
Fresh thyme
Bay leaves
1 carrot, diced
½ cup Dry Sack sherry
½ pound sweet butter
Salt to taste

Slice each breast into 4 pieces and arrange parsley in a small ball in center of serving platter, placing sliced breasts around it. Lay legs across top with chanterelles around. Complete by covering entire dish with sauce.

Sauce

Sauté bones in oil until they turn brown. Add pepper, shallots, thyme, bay leaves, and carrot. Cook for 3 minutes. Drain excess grease. Add the Dry Sack, and cover with water. Cook additional 15 minutes. Drain the sauce and reduce. Add butter, incorporating slowly while whipping sauce. Add salt and pepper to taste.

NOTE: When the Hyatt was asked for something that could be shared with any chef, no matter how remote the area, they immediately sent their recipe for chocolate chip cookies.

Chocolate Chip Cookies

Makes 2 dozen

In a state well known for its audacious brags, the Hyatt Regency chefs boast of their chocolate chip cookies: "They are said to be the best in Texas by some of our regular guests!" If the elegant and flamboyant Hyatt is not in your price range, you can now at least make your own decision as to the excellent quality of their chocolate chip cookies.

1 cup shortening
1 cup granulated sugar
¾ cup brown sugar
3 eggs
3 cups bread flour
2 teaspoons salt
1½ teaspoons baking powder
1 teaspoon vanilla
2 cups chopped pecans
4 cups (1 pound) semisweet chocolate chips

Cream shortening and add sugars. Add eggs and mix well. Add dry ingredients and mix. Add vanilla and pecans and mix. Add chocolate, but mix only to combine. Bake at 325° on greased cookie sheet for 20 minutes.

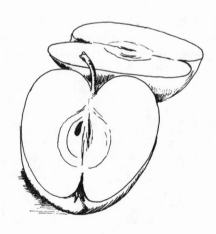

Shrimp Regency

Serves 4

The state dish of Texas may be chili, but another overwhelming Lone Star favorite is shrimp. Fry them, boil them, stuff them, or prepare them just about any other way, and Texans love this saltwater delicacy. The Hyatt's Shrimp Regency was introduced by Ed Keeling to the Hyatt restaurant on Sunset in Hollywood. It was the favorite item on the menu and outsold everything else. The Crystal Cactus Restaurant expects the same smashing results in Fort Worth. Even though the recipe is imported, the main ingredients are homegrown — somewhere off that long Texas coastline.

4 ounces sweet butter
20 jumbo shrimp, peeled and deveined
Flour
2 cloves garlic, diced
1 bunch green onions, sliced thin
3 whole tomatoes, peeled and diced
1 shallot, diced
1 cup sherry
1 cup Chardonnay white wine
Salt and pepper to taste
8 ounces cocktail sauce
8 ounces mushrooms, sliced
2 cups heavy cream
Juice of 2 lemons

Heat butter, but be careful not to brown. Dredge shrimp in flour and place in hot butter. Add garlic, green onions, tomatoes, and shallots, and simmer until garlic starts to brown. Add sherry and white wine. Salt and pepper to taste. Keep stirring and add cocktail sauce and mushrooms. Add heavy cream, and when it begins to thicken, add lemon juice. When shrimp start to curl, they are done.

Salmon Timbale with Ratatouille

Serves 4

Ratatouille originated in the Provence region of France. This eggplant, tomato, and squash dish is served with all manner of meats, but it is especially appetizing with lamb and fish. *Timbale* is also a French word for kettledrum, so obviously the eggplant medley will be served in a bowl of salmon.

The Crystal Cactus Restaurant's menu offers this exciting nouvelle cuisine dish because it is not only a gourmet specialty but also low in cholesterol and calories, yet has many important minerals and vitamins. This is truly a dieter's delight!

4 red peppers
1 yellow pepper
1 green pepper
1 zucchini
½ onion
1 eggplant
Sweet butter
16 ounces salmon
Salt
White pepper
1 teaspoon basil
2 tomatoes
2 ounces chicken stock
2 ounces olive oil

Cut two red peppers and the green and yellow peppers in half and clean out. Roast in oven until skin peels off easily. Slice zucchini, onion, and eggplant wafer thin. Sauté in sweet butter until tender. Place all vegetables on a towel to soak up excess moisture. Slice salmon paper thin.

Take a soup cup and brush the inside with olive oil. Cover sides and bottom with salmon, leaving enough to overlap rim with about 1 inch hanging over the sides. Sprinkle with a little salt, white pepper, and basil. Peel tomatoes and slice off the meat. Layer the timbale, pushing firmly between layers:

zucchini
tomatoes
green pepper
red pepper
onion
eggplant
yellow pepper

Fold over excess salmon and press down firmly to make sure all ingredients are tightly packed.

Sauce

Place the two leftover red peppers in a blender and puree until fine. Add chicken stock. Add salt and white pepper to taste. Slowly add olive oil.

Place the timbale in a pan half-filled with water. Bake in a preheated 350° oven for 10 to 12 minutes. Keep the salmon a little rare, and do not allow to dry out.

Cover the bottom of a plate with sauce. Take out the timbale. Run a paring knife around the rim to loosen and take the timbale out. Slice the timbale down the middle, and slide apart halfway to reveal the insides. Pour on the sauce. Garnish with leftover diced tomatoes on top with a whole basil leaf sticking out.

Kincaid Hotel
Uvalde

After the Revolution, both Texas and Mexico claimed the territory between the Nueces River and the Rio Grande, so the Nueces Strip became a veritable paradise for renegades of both nations. Finally, a fast gun named King Fisher took control of the wild and wooly strip, and King managed to evade justice and the Texas Rangers as well. Fisher came to the end of his sordid career in a gunfight in Austin. Buried in the town he controlled, he lies in Uvalde not far from his famous sign, "This is King Fisher's road. Take the other."

Uvalde's colorful citizens did not end with Fisher. After collecting his $500 reward for the demise of Billy the Kid, Pat Garrett moved to Uvalde and became an avid horse racer and friend of John Nance Garner. For about sixteen years, Pat made Uvalde his home, until he returned to New Mexico only to be shot by Wayne Brazil.

Vice-presidents of the United States are often forgotten figures of history, but John Nance Garner was the first Texan to be elected speaker of the House and then vice-president under FDR. Garner did not agree with Roosevelt's bid for a third term and resigned as a running mate. On a quiet shady street in Uvalde, Garner's home is now a marvelous little museum of his life and political career.

With its historic past, Uvalde has some wonderful old buildings. The opera house has been beautifully restored, and across the street on the square is the Kincaid Hotel, built in 1927. Begun by a wealthy rancher, W. D. Kincaid, the hotel was completed after his death as a memorial by his widow and children. Its lobby decked out with longhorn heads and handsome furniture, the Kincaid was the social hub of Uvalde. At its completion, the hotel had the only electric elevator between San Antonio and El Paso to take guests to their $1.50 rooms.

Since its construction the Kincaid has had many owners, and as has been the case for nearly all small-town hotels, hard times arrived. An attempt to convert the hotel into apartments failed, and even a new facade added in the 1960s did not bring prosperity. The Kincaid is once again open as a hotel, and the small lobby is very nice with its Victorian pieces. The elevator still creaks up four stories as it carries guests to rooms that are clean and inexpensive, but none is furnished in antiques.

Many famous guests have signed the Kincaid's register. With the perfect set for Hollywood westerns just down the road at Brackettville, movie stars as Dana Andrews, Richard Widmark, and Ronald Reagan came to Uvalde. Eddie Rickenbacker came here, as did several Texas governors and President Lyndon Johnson. In the 1940s a reception was held in the Kincaid's Crystal Ballroom honoring Mrs. Harry S. Truman and her daughter Margaret. The Western Union desk in the lobby handled the hundreds of congratulatory telegrams when Uvalde's favorite son, "Cactus Jack" Garner, celebrated his ninetieth birthday.

In spite of its numerous owners and alterations, the old Kincaid is certainly worthy of its Texas Historical Medallion.

Tostadas and Nachos

Tostadas are a favorite "bar food" or appetizer before Texans heap their plates with frijoles, tacos, enchiladas, chalupas, and all those other Mexican dishes so loved by residents of the Lone Star state. For something a bit fancier and more filling, cheese and jalapeños make a spicy nacho. You don't really need a recipe for these simple nibbles, but if you are a novice at Mexican food, Mr. Flores at the Kincaid suggests the way folks in Uvalde like their tostadas and nachos.

Cut fresh or canned corn tortillas into triangles and deep fry in hot oil until crisp. Drain on paper towels. Sprinkle with salt. These are the original corn chips and good with dips, soups, or beverages.

For nachos, prepare the tortillas as above. While they are still hot, sprinkle with onion or garlic salt and chili powder. Or sprinkle the chips with grated longhorn cheese, chili powder, and garlic salt. Heat in oven until cheese is melted, and then top each chip with a small slice of jalapeño pepper. Or top with pepper before placing in oven. *¡Viva México!*

72

Chiles Rellenos

Serves 4

The Kincaid Hotel Coffee Shop is a downtown Uvalde tradition, and the chef, Mr. Fausto Flores, has been turning out his Mexican specialties for the Kincaid's customers for more than twenty-five years.

8 green chilies
1 cup Monterey Jack cheese, cubed
½ cup flour
½ teaspoon salt
2 eggs, beaten
Cooking oil

Select full-bodied, firm, straight chilies, allowing 2 per person. Wash and dry. Cut the tip end from each pod to prevent its bursting.

To roast and peel, slit pods lengthwise and remove seeds and veins. Place pods on a cookie sheet under broiler. Turn frequently. Allow to blister (but not burn) on each side. Remove and cover with a damp towel for 10 minutes. Then peel skins from stem downward.

Fill each chili pepper with cheese. Roll in mixture of flour and salt. Dip in beaten eggs. Fry in moderately hot oil until golden brown.

Note: While much tastier if made with fresh green peppers, this recipe was tested also with canned chilies, and it was delicious.

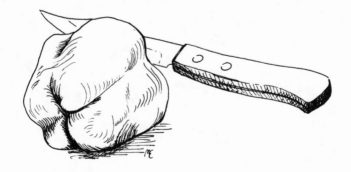

Frijoles

Serves 8

There probably are as many ways of cooking this all-time Texas favorite staple as there are recipes for chili. Endless discussions take place among cooks as the best way to prepare pintos. The basic ingredient, of course, is dried beans. However, if you are lucky enough to be at a farmers' market in a big city in the spring, these wonderful beans can be obtained fresh in the shell. And fresh-cooked pinto beans are absolutely magnificent, no matter what seasoning you use. Alas, the season is short, and Texans must have their frijoles all year, so here is how Mr. Flores of the Kincaid serves his customers.

> 3 cups dried pinto beans
> 4 quarts water
> 1 clove garlic, peeled
> 1 cup salt pork, diced
> Salt

Wash beans well and remove "rocks." Cover with water and soak overnight. Drain. Cover with fresh water, add garlic and salt pork, but *not* salt. Cover pot tightly and bring to a boil. Reduce heat and simmer for 1½ hours or until beans are tender but not mushy. Add boiling water during cooking if necessary and stir occasionally. When beans are done, remove lid, turn up heat, and cook until all liquid has been absorbed. Add salt to taste.

La Borde House

Rio Grande City

Some of the most fascinating features in Texas are its many anachronisms. Travelers in Texas often find a totally unexpected attraction. One of the best examples of this phenomenon can be found on the hot dusty banks of the Rio Grande River. One would hardly expect to find a building that is appropriate for the elegant New Orleans French Quarter in a town on the Texas-Mexico border, but thanks to Larry Sheerin of San Antonio, one of the most impressive historic inns in Texas is the La Borde House in Rio Grande City.

According to the story, a Frenchman named François La Borde forgot to leave his sternwheeler at McAllen and ended up in Rio Grande City. This was back in the late 1880s when the Rio Grande was the main highway, and Rio Grande City was one of its most important ports of call. La Borde fared well as a merchant and journeyed to Paris to commission French architects to design his Texas home. The result was a mixture of Creole, Texan, and Victorian features that set the La Borde home apart from any other structure on the river.

The railroad arrived, and with all the traffic up and down the border, La Borde converted his home and store into a hotel. Then, for some unexplained reason, this apparently successful businessman committed suicide.

In the early 1930s the property was acquired by a geologist, George Boyle, and La Borde House became the Ringgold Hotel, named for historic Fort Ringgold on the outskirts of town. The clientele of the Ringgold were certainly varied and of many professions. Sheerin tells the story of how one of Rio Grande City's ladies of the evening kept her accounts posted on the walls of her room. Fortunately, her "books" were never audited, or some well-known citizens might have been found on her list of IOUs.

77

Today, with large sums invested by Sheerin in its restoration, La Borde House is absolutely exquisite. Robert Kendall of Dallas turned the Ringgold into the epitome of elegant inns. As you sit in its Victorian parlor surrounded by gorgeous antiques, George Boyle will be delighted to entertain you with amusing anecdotes of the hotel and the area. Or you can relax in one of several patio retreats, sip a cool refreshment, and listen to fountains tinkle their soft melodies. Not only does the harried world of city life seem millions of miles away, but if you look at the map, you actually *are* a long way from freeways and traffic jams.

The historic rooms are complete with canopy beds, massive wardrobes, charming sofas, and claw-foot tubs. As it was in days past, the pedestal lavatory is part of the bedroom's furniture. Behind the historic part of La Borde House is a row of contemporary efficiency apartments that are very popular during hunting season.

The manager of La Borde House is Che Guerra, and the restaurant is named for this tall, handsome young man. Che's is as beautifully decorated as the rest of the historic hotel is, and the menu is typical of the area. One of the most beautiful rooms, the Bluebonnet Room, had to be sacrificed to accommodate the bar and restaurant; but the result is worth it. Now there are two wonderful reasons to go to Rio Grande City—the La Borde House and Che's.

Kenny's Bean Soup

Serves 12

Kenny is the chef at Che's, and here is his version of the Texas border favorite (and a favorite of the rest of Texas as well).

2 pounds pinto beans
¼ pound salt pork
1 small onion, chopped
1 tomato, chopped
2 serrano peppers, chopped
1 cup cilantro, chopped

Boil beans with salt pork 2 hours. Add all spices except cilantro. Cook 1 hour more. Thirty minutes before serving, add the cilantro and cook.

Tamale Pie

Yields 3 9-inch pies

While Larry Sheerin was adding Che's Restaurant to the exquisite La Borde House, whenever he was asked what was going to be the menu, he always replied, "Border cuisine." That means steak, chicken-fried steak, and Mexican food. However, those three all-time great Texas favorites are certainly not limited to the border. And Che's Tamale Pie definitely needs to be shared with Texans a long way from the Rio Grande.

12 slices bacon
2 pounds ground beef
2 cups whole-kernel corn, drained
½ cup green chilies, chopped
1 cup green onions, chopped
½ cup cornmeal
2 teaspoons ground red chilies
1 teaspoon salt
1 teaspoon black pepper
1 teaspoon ground comino
16 ounces tomato sauce
½ cup stuffed green olives, chopped
3 9-inch pie crusts

Fry bacon and set aside. Brown beef and drain. Stir in remaining ingredients and pour into pie crusts. Bake at 425° for 25 minutes.

Topping
4 eggs
1½ cups evaporated milk
3 teaspoons dry mustard
3 cups Monterey Jack cheese, grated

Combine ingredients and spread on baked pie. Crumble bacon on top and bake 5 minutes more at 425°. Let firm before serving.

La Colombe d'Or
Houston

La Colombe d'Or, translated "The Golden Dove," epitomizes the philosophy of *joie de vivre*. A brainchild of Houston developer and lawyer Steve Zimmerman, this French auberge features the best continental cuisine, aged wines, and impeccable hospitality. It is Houston's contribution to the European hotel tradition, and this was the owner's intent. Steve, a native of New Orleans, has made traveling through Europe a way of life. Known as the "King of Montrose," he says that his New Orleans background and his travels abroad "deepened my interest in some of those things that make life worth living: food, wine, and art."

Particularly influenced by the Auberge Colombe d'Or in St. Paul de Vence, a village in Provence in the hills above Nice, Steve has patterned his own hotel after this French Riviera retreat. The original Colombe d'Or has been a favorite of artists, actors, writers, and royalty-in-exile for years. It features an art collection from young struggling artists who paid for room and board with their paintings. Today, these paintings still hang there; now, however, such names as Miró, Chagall, and Picasso are recognized as being great. Movie buffs would also be interested in knowing that Yves Montand and Simone Signoret were married there. At any rate, Steve had his model, and Houston now has a little bit of the French Riviera practically within walking distance of downtown.

The mansion itself has a history all its own. Built on the fashionable Montrose thoroughfare in 1923 by Walter Fondren, founder of Humble Oil, the 12,000-square-foot gold-brown brick residence was designed by Houston architect Alfred C. Finn, who also created the Gulf Building, the Rice Hotel, and the San Jacinto Monument. The house was recorded on the National Register, and the Fondren family continued to live there until the mid-1950s. When the surviving Mrs. Fondren moved to River

Oaks, she allowed the American Red Cross to use the mansion free of charge for many years. They apparently didn't appreciate the home's interior, since they were quick to cover the ornate molded ceiling with acoustical tile and hide hardwood floors with linoleum. To utilize every square foot, spacious rooms were separated by plasterboard walls to make smaller offices.

The Montrose neighborhood began its decline after World War II. Pawnshops, used-car lots, and bars began to crop up, and the entire area became dilapidated. Then, around 1970, a few professionals like Steve began to show interest in the area, and Montrose thus experienced a renaissance. It is now chic by most standards, with its boutiques, art galleries, and restaurants.

La Colombe d'Or has it all: a good location, a worldly proprietor, and a colorful past. With Steve's direction and with the stylish decor provided by Beta Tau Alpha when the mansion was the 1980 Designers' Showhouse, the hotel and restaurant became a place of style and affluence without ostentation. The sunny dining room, for example, is decorated with contemporary paintings by Houston artists. The lobby is striking with its intricate parquet floor of maple, cherry, mahogany, and oak. Be sure to have a glass of cognac in the Victorian library or wander into the cozy walnut bar for a quick nightcap. Then be prepared to be impressed with the second and third floors, where overnight guests are lavished with all the European amenities. You will find five suites on the second level, each with its own dining room, and one sleeping porch. Furnished with king-sized beds, the rooms sport a mauve, neutral, and coral decor that differs from suite to suite with such accents as Art Nouveau glass light shades, original brass faucets in bathrooms, and styles ranging from Whistlerian Oriental to Prince Albert modern. Such touches as the painted flocks of roseate spoonbills that adorn the walls of a suite's dining room or the antique Chinese celadon reflect Steve's love of art. Even the suites are named after Monet, Cézanne, Renoir, Degas, and Van Gogh.

Be prepared as a hotel guest to get the royal treatment. A decanter of wine, along with chocolates, fresh fruit, and flowers, will be waiting for you when you check into your room. In the morning, enjoy a hot cup of coffee or tea in your own sunny dining room, as well as freshly squeezed orange juice, a basket of flaky French croissants, strawberry jam, and undyed butter. Read your complimentary *Houston Post* and *Wall Street Journal* as you ponder world affairs. There's one thing for sure: your $150- to $400-a-night room will provide you with a quiet atmosphere in which to do all the thinking you want. If money is indeed no object, stay in the 2,000-square-foot penthouse, a wonder among wonders complete with whirlpool, formal dining room, bedroom, and bath, and facilities for private parties from two to two hundred. Further amenities include secretarial service, laundry by hand, and twenty-four hour concierge.

But be sure to return in time for lunch or dinner in the restaurant. Delight in the cream of cauliflower soup, or for a taste of the Côte d'Azur, try the Soupe de Poisson. Then go on to the Scampi Colombe d'Or or Carré d'Agneaux. For a delightful dessert, the Brulée is a must.

Though La Colombe d'Or has been called the nation's smallest luxury hotel, there is nothing small about its ambience, which certainly equals the great chateaus of France.

Crème Brulée

Serves 4 to 6

Brulée, a smooth New Orleans dessert, is a favorite of proprietor Steve Zimmerman. This secret recipe was given to Steve by a good friend of his who owns a well-known restaurant in New Orleans.

  1 quart whipping cream
10 egg yolks
  1 teaspoon vanilla extract
  4 ounces superfine sugar
  8 ounces brown sugar

Heat whipping cream until warm. Remove from heat and beat in mixing bowl. In another mixing bowl whip egg yolks and then mix in vanilla and sugar. After this has been mixed well, add whipping cream. Pour in ovenproof one-serving containers and bake at 300° for 1 hour in a bath of water. Remove from oven and cool. Top with brown sugar and brown under broiler until sugar forms crunchy topping.

Cream of Cauliflower Soup

Serves 20

1 pound fresh butter
1 head of leek, white part, chopped fine
1 yellow onion, chopped fine
3 heads of cauliflower, cut into small pieces
1 gallon chicken stock
Salt and pepper to taste
1 quart whipping cream

Put 8 ounces butter in a soup pot and heat. Add leek and onion and sauté until onion turns brown. Add cauliflower and sauté for 10 to 15 minutes. Add chicken stock. Cook until boiling. Reduce heat and cook for 1 hour. Strain all vegetables and continue to cook broth over low heat. Finely chop all vegetables in food processor, return to chicken broth, and cook for 30 minutes. Add salt, pepper, whipping cream, and 8 ounces butter mixed well. Mix with soup until just heated.

Chicken Stock
3 to 4 chicken bones
1 bunch celery
3 to 4 carrots
2 yellow onions
1 head of leek
2 to 3 bay leaves
Dash thyme

Combine all ingredients and cook 1 hour or more. Strain before using.

Scampi Colombe d'Or

Serves 2

Shrimp Scampi originated in New Orleans, the city of the Blues, Bourbon Street, and booze. They are prepared in such a way, however, that you needed to wear a bib and peel the shrimp yourself. Steve decided to upgrade the recipe and peel the shrimp, "keeping the sauce spicy and adding cream." *Chef de cuisine* Hervé Glin prepares the shrimp to suit even the most discerning palate. A native of Brittany, Chef Glin trained in Brest, then joined the staff of the famed Pied de Cochon restaurant in Paris. Glin came to the New World to ply his trade in Montreal at the Four Seasons Hotel, then moved to Houston with the boom to settle in as *chef de cuisine* at the Colombe d'Or.

6 large scampi
2 ounces butter
2 ounces white wine
Ground black pepper to taste
1 clove freshly chopped garlic
1 cup whipping cream

Bake scampi in individual ovenproof dishes with 1 ounce butter and 1 ounce white wine at 375° for 15 to 20 minutes. Do not overcook! Pour sauce on top of cooked scampi and serve with fresh vegetables such as asparagus and snow pea pods.

Scampi Sauce

Over low heat, cook 1 ounce white wine and black pepper until half evaporated. Add whipping cream at low heat until mixture becomes thick. Remove from heat. In another pan, sauté 1 ounce butter and garlic; cook until brown. Add cream mixture and all remaining butter and salt to taste.

Lamplighter
Inn
Floydada

Hotels rarely had romantic names during the era of trains and traveling salesmen; the Lamplighter Inn began its career in 1913 with the very functional name of Commercial Hotel. Mr. and Mrs. William Daily catered to drummers. All three meals were hearty affairs, served on starched white linen, and lunch and dinner were often three or four courses. A Texas-sized steak cost 25 cents.

Mr. Daily "fetched" the drummers from the railroad station in his horse and buggy rig, and they set up their wares in the spacious hotel lobby. Local merchants arrived to place their orders for farm implements, dry goods, hardware, and patent medicines. Catalogs were not the way to do business then, and of course without the traveling salesmen, we wouldn't have all those jokes about the farmer's daughter.

The hotel has remained in the Daily family, and today it is run by their granddaughter, Dorothy Hotchkiss. Originally thirty-two rooms were available for guests, but now fourteen are open, with twelve baths. There is no longer any drop-in trade; overnight guests are accepted by reservation only. Much of the hotel's 1913 furniture, linens, and bedding are still in use, and the lobby with its pressed tin ceiling is delightful. The Lamplighter Inn is a great favorite for local family reunions.

If you are heading north out of Lubbock, detour east for a few miles and visit John and Dorothy at the Lamplighter Inn. If Floydada is not exactly on your route to somewhere, you can still share their hospitality with Dorothy's recipes for grits and peanut brittle, both good old Texas fare.

Hot Cheese Grits

Serves 30

You simply cannot find a more southern dish than grits. Those Yankees who come down South often turn up their noses at one of the best foods that ever originated in America. What would a slice of tender fried ham be without grits and redeye gravy? Some prefer grits with their breakfast eggs, because Mother always served them that way. And there is nothing better than a bowl of grits with melted butter and a touch of salt to start the day. There is quite an art to cooking grits so they aren't too watery and certainly not lumpy. The exact consistency may take a few practice cookings, but once you get the knack, you'll "Kiss My Grits!"

Grits have also become sophisticated. Here is Dorothy's recipe with sherry and green chilies.

2 cups quick grits
8 cups boiling water
1 teaspoon salt
1½ sticks magarine
8 ounces Kraft hot jalapeño cheese
16 ounces Kraft garlic cheese
2 eggs, beaten
2 tablespoons sherry
1 teaspoon Lea & Perrins Worcestershire sauce
1 teaspoon Tabasco sauce
2 12-ounce cans green chilies, chopped

Slowly stir grits into boiling salted water. Turn heat off. Add margarine and cheese to grits mixture. Cool.

Add eggs, sherry, Lea & Perrins, Tabasco, and chilies. Spoon mixture into greased baking dish and bake 1 hour at 300°.

Note: This freezes well. Water will appear on top, but just remix and reheat. Superb with ham or chicken.

Peanut Brittle

Yields 1 pound

- 1½ cups sugar
- ½ cup light Karo syrup
- ¼ cup boiling water
- 1½ cups raw peanuts
- 1½ teaspoons baking soda

Mix sugar, Karo, and water in heavy skillet. Heat and stir until sugar is dissolved. Add peanuts. Over medium heat, stir mixture occasionally from sides toward the middle. When a light tan syrup (amber, not dark) forms, remove from heat and stir in soda immediately. Pour onto buttered cookie sheet. Break into those hunks of candy that bring back memories of growing up.

The
Lancaster
Houston

If you are a lover of the finer things in life, you'll be happy to know that your every need will be met in downtown Houston's cultural center. You can hear the Houston Symphony at Jones Hall or see a play at the Alley Theatre and then eat a romantic midnight meal at the Lancaster Grille. Should you decide to stay in town overnight, sleep at the very European, very posh Lancaster Hotel, once called the Auditorium Hotel. For those old-timers who remember the old Auditorium, a 1926 hotel located across the street from its namesake (the City Auditorium), its $18 million renovation was like having an old friend get a complete face-lift. A moderately priced 200-room hotel, the old establishment was a meeting place for theater stars, athletes (top-billed wrestlers from City Auditorium came here), and World War II servicemen who stayed here because of the Circus Club, a USO entertainment center. Dupree Fountain, the hotel's first owner and manager, stated that the Auditorium was "Houston's new all-modern hotel with two double speed elevators, circulating ice water and ceiling fans in every room." A 1926 news article reported that the twelve-story Auditorium replaced a wooden building, transforming what was one of Texas Avenue's most unsightly corners into an attractive spot.

Today the old shell has been totally restored, and the hotel now houses 84 roomy guest quarters and 10 suites. The brick exterior has been painted, highlighted by terra cotta cornices and trimmed with new eight-paned windows installed throughout the entire hotel. Large multipaned showcase windows covered by burgundy awnings are at the front, with colorful flags and flower boxes situated below windows in true European style. Cut stones for sidewalks around the hotel add to the European motif.

The hotel's interior is decorated in nineteenth-century antiques and oil paintings. Its owners, the Lancaster Partners, Limited, totally gutted floors two through twelve and designed each room so that every one is unique in layout. The marble staircase leading to the mezzanine level was refurbished, and all the floors are parquet and marble. There are brass accessories, custom rugs, and fresh flowers. All wallpapers and draperies were imported from England, and the custom furniture in each room includes a working desk and upholstered easy chairs and ottomans. Doors are solid wood with brass knockers and peepholes for security. Bathrooms are designed with imported Italian marble vanities and floors, wraparound mirrors, brass fixtures, and cast-iron tubs. Guest amenities are in abundance at the Lancaster, including a basket of toiletries and plush towels. Linda Hudson, the general manager, gives an indication of the hotel's philosophy when she says, "We place such amenities as a terry-cloth robe, an umbrella, late edition magazines, bottled sparkling water, and three to four telephones in each room." There is also a full-time concierge, a manager-in-residence, valet service, bed turndown service, and limousine service, to name a few features.

As for the food served in the Lancaster Grill, it is absolutely wonderful. With executive chef Henry Pile in command, the cuisine ranges from grilled salmon to poached chicken breast to lamb chops. Try the onion soup, served in a bread roll instead of a bowl. The Lancaster's fare is truly elegant, but one would expect nothing less from Chef Pile, a graduate of the Culinary Institute of America. He has been associated with such restaurants as New York's famous "21" Club, the Adam's Mark Hotel in Houston, and the Sea Turtle Inn and Restaurant in Atlantic Beach, Florida. The recipes that follow are Chef Pile's.

Sautéed Snow Peas with Sesame

Serves 4 to 6

2 tablespoons vegetable oil
1 pound snow peas, trimmed and stringed
2 tablespoons sesame oil
1 tablespoon seasame seeds, toasted
Salt and white pepper to taste

Heat oil in sauté pan until almost smoking. Add snow peas and sauté quickly over high heat until just tender. Add sesame oil and sesame seeds; toss very quickly and season with salt and white pepper.

Julienne of Carrot with Ginger and Honey

Serves 6

4 tablespoons butter
1 pound carrots, peeled and cut into fine julienne
2 tablespoons fresh ginger, grated
2 tablespoons honey
Salt to taste

Melt butter in sauté pan. Add carrot julienne and ginger. Sauté over moderately high heat until carrots are *just* tender. Add honey and salt to taste.

Grilled Salmon Filet with Caper Butter

Serves 4

4 6-ounce salmon filets
Salt and white pepper
1 stick sweet butter, softened
1 teaspoon parsley, chopped
1 shallot, chopped very fine
1 teaspoon chives, chopped
Lemon juice
Black pepper
1 tablespoon capers

Season fish with salt and white pepper. Brush lightly with oil to prevent salmon from sticking to grill. Place oiled and seasoned salmon filets under a hot broiler for 30 seconds before placing on grill.

Grill fish until just done. It is done when a finger pressed against the filet can feel the sections of the fish slice slightly against each other.

Place filet on plate, top with 1 tablespoon of butter, and place under a hot broiler until butter is just melted.

Butter

Combine all ingredients except capers. Blend in food processor. Fold in capers.

Serve salmon garnished with parsley sprigs and slices of lemon.

Landmark
Inn
Castroville

For centuries, Germany and France have squabbled over Alsace-Lorraine, and whichever country was in power at the time took this disputed territory as its own. But the Alsatians had their own particular traditions and loyalties, and they spoke their own unrecorded language. Unique not only in Texas but also in the United States, a group of these unusual colonists brought a bit of the River Rhine to the River Medina in tiny Castroville.

In 1842 a French Jew of Spanish and Portuguese ancestry named Henri Castro secured a land grant from the struggling young Republic of Texas. Anxious to prevent Mexican infiltration of its sparsely settled lands, Texas was eager for the Jewish impresario's colonization plans. Like most grandiose schemers, Castro was plagued with problems, and it was not until 1844 that he arrived with his settlers. Life was far from easy on the raw Texas frontier, but in spite of hostile Indians and devastating cholera, the Alsatians endured. Their homes were built in their particular European style with asymmetrical roof lines, and as much of Alsace as possible was transported to Texas.

A few years after Castroville was founded, a stagecoach stop was erected for San Antonio–bound travelers. Soon the station evolved into an inn, and the Vance Hotel became as steeped in Texas history as Castroville had been. In addition to the inn, the complex consisted of a general store, a gristmill, and a bathhouse. According to tradition, the lead lining of the bathhouse was used to make bullets for Confederate guns.

When the railroad bypassed Castroville, so did progress. Fortunately for Texas, this unusual little town has remained almost unchanged. Today, busy U.S. Highway 90 races through Castroville, bringing tourists and prosperity, for the outside world has fallen in love with this quaint bit of Europe. Antique stores are doing a big business, and also back in business is the Vance Hotel, now the Landmark Inn.

A generous gift to the state of Texas by its former owner, Mrs. Ruth

Lawler, the old stage stop is one of the most popular hostelries in Texas. Some of its eight rooms share baths. There is no television or air-conditioning, and the furnishings are a mixture of antiques and the 1940s styles, but the Landmark is booked solid almost every night.

Good food and feasting are age-old Alsatian traditions, so part of the charm of Castroville is dining on superb fare at McVay's Alsatian Restaurant or savoring the breads and pastries at Haby's Alsatian Bakery.

Peach Cobbler

Serves 8

Georgia is not the only state famous for its fine peaches, because the Texas Hill Country has some of the best orchards in the nation. When the fruit begins to ripen, signs line many Hill Country roads saying, "Pick Your Own Peaches Here!" If picking your own doesn't appeal to you, the roads are also lined with local folks bringing their luscious, sweet, rosy peaches to you.

Naturally, when fresh peaches are available the favorite dessert is fresh peach cobbler. At the Alsatian Restaurant, Lora Mae McVay has come up with a simple cobbler guaranteed to please the most discriminating lovers of cobbler.

> 5 cups sugar
> ¼ teaspoon salt
> ¾ cup flour
> 1 gallon fresh peaches, peeled and cut up
> Dash mace
> As much butter as you can spare

Mix flour, salt, and sugar together. Then mix with fruit. Pour into large flat pan. Cover with pie crust. Sprinkle on a little more sugar and some mace. Dot with butter. Bake at 350° until golden brown.

Original St. Louis Day Coleslaw

Serves 6 to 8

The beautiful Gothic church in Castroville is the third St. Louis church on this site and is the result of the work of a dedicated priest, Father Peter Richard. On August 25, 1870, special services were celebrated for the first time as the sun streamed through the beautiful stained-glass windows. Each year, on the Sunday closest to August 25, Castrovillians honor this memorable service with a festival that proves how dearly Alsatians love good food and drink. St. Louis Day draws thousands of visitors.

The townsfolk prepare a giant Alsatian sausage and barbeque meal, and family recipes are featured at the numerous food booths scattered throughout Koenig Park. If you can't be in Castroville for this memorable feast, you can share the original coleslaw as prepared by Lora Mae McVay at the Alsatian Restaurant.

1 large head cabbage, shredded very fine
1 onion, chopped
1 green pepper, chopped
20 stuffed olives
1 cup sugar

Combine first four ingredients and pour sugar over vegetables. Let stand 15 minutes.

Dressing
1 cup white vinegar
1 tablespoon celery seed
½ cup salad oil
1 tablespoon salt
1 tablespoon prepared mustard

Combine ingredients and pour over vegetables.

Alsatian Pastada (Meat Pie)

Makes 3 9-inch pies

There are many ethnic versions of a meat pie, and this Alsatian *pastada* arrived in Texas with the first settlers who established Castroville. Simple and hearty, it is a main course that is certain to please.

6 pounds lean pork, chopped
4 large onions, chopped
1 handful fresh parsley
3 tablespoons granulated garlic or 3 cloves fresh
2 tablespoons sugar
Red cooking wine

Put all ingredients except sugar and wine together in a large covered pot. Just cover the meat with half water and half wine. Add sugar. Cook slowly for at least 2 hours and until liquid is reduced to half. Remove from heat and pour into unbaked pie shells. Cover top with pie crust. Bake until nice and brown at 350° (about 20 minutes).

Haby's Alsatian Bakery

The bakery was opened in its present location on January 10, 1959. The original baker was John Gries, an immigrant who came from Berlin in the early 1920s. Stanley Haby went to work for Mr. Gries in 1939 and bought the business from him in 1940. The bakery and cafe were in a building across the street from the present Zion Lutheran Church.

Sammy and Yvonne Tschirhart purchased the bakery from Stanley and Ella Haby when the Habys retired. They remodeled the building and increased the variety of products. In 1983 they completed a major expansion, with architecture patterned after old Alsace. The half-timbered or *fachwerk* effect, steep red roof, and dormer windows were copied from pictures of old buildings in Alsace that the Tschirharts collected during their travels.

The following anise cookies can be found in most bakeries in Alsace. The recipe was given to them by a friend from D'Hanis, but the ratio of ingredients is the same as that given by a baker in Zellenberg.

Anise Cookies

Yields 18 dozen

6 eggs
3 cups sugar
1 teaspoon anise oil (you'll need to go to an old-fashioned drugstore
for this ingredient)
3 cups flour
Anise seed

Stir eggs 30 minutes. (You'll need a strong arm for this. Sammy and
Yvonne suggest that you do not beat.) Add sugar and beat for 30 minutes.
Add anise oil and flour. Then add anise seed to taste. Drop on wax paper.
Let dry overnight. Bake approximately 20 minutes at 225° to 250°.

Molasses Cookies

Yields 39 dozen

Making molasses was once a regular summer ritual, and it was the
sweetener that was used by the early settlers. As sugar became more
readily available, people stopped making molasses because it involved
much hard work. First there was stripping and cutting the cane. Then
the cane was pressed and the juice cooked five to six hours over a wood
fire. In the last several years, however, there has been a revival of the
old-time method. Sammy and Yvonne make their own molasses;
however, you can still use store-bought for the following recipe:

4½ pounds sugar
2 ounces salt
2 pounds, 4 ounces shortening
¾ gallon molasses
3 ounces soda
1 quart milk
11 pounds flour
1½ pounds nuts

Mix together and bake at 350° until done.
This recipe will make enough cookies to feed the entire town of
Castroville!

Lickskillet
Inn
Fayetteville

Living in the city these days is learning to live with traffic, smog, and a frantic pace that is guaranteed to set the most placid individual on edge. One of the best ways to mend those frazzled nerves is to get away to a pleasant, quiet, peaceful, and restful retreat. For a perfect vacation, head out for tiny Fayetteville, a Czech community caught in time, where no one is making any misguided efforts to "rescue" it from its time warp.

There is not much to do in Fayetteville, but that's the reason you go there. You can stroll around the square and sip a brew at the funky beer joint with the odd name of Schramm's Confectionary, buy an antique or two, and admire the courthouse. If you are into graves, visit the cemetery, a treasure of old tombstones, complete with photographs of the deceased.

The complete the bucolic weekend, stay at the Lickskillet Inn. Steve and Jeanette Donaldson have turned their historic cottage into a quaint down-home inn. The small white house features a picket fence, swings on the porch, a hammock in the yard, and a fat dog spread-eagle in the doorway. Rooms are filled with Jeanette's little personal touches, such as old knickknacks, antique furniture and beds, and even a real working potbellied stove. In authentic detail, the bath is at the end of the hall.

The Donaldsons named their inn for Fayetteville's original moniker. Back in the early 1800s, communities held get-togethers to work on various projects. One of the big attractions for workers was the abundance of good food. Late arrivals often found all the "fixin's" gone and were told they would just have to "lick the skillet clean." So, before Fayetteville got an official name, it was just Lickskillet, Texas.

At the Donaldsons' version of Lickskillet, the "fixin's" are simple but delicious. Since this is also their home, a restaurant would never fit in; but you can certainly "lick the skillet clean" on some of the Donaldsons' breakfast fare.

Part of the fun of staying with the Donaldsons is gathering around the dining-room table for the continental breakfast and making new friends. Jeanette, also known as "Goldie," serves beer bread with jams, jellies, and honey accompanied by fruit in season and coffee or tea. With this also come shared stories and experiences from the interesting guests who love the informal atmosphere at the inn.

Goldie says, "I learned to make the beer bread while cooking for fifty people on the Salt Grass Trail Ride. Most of the cooking was done on the open fire, and I really enjoyed the two years I worked my way over the seven-day trip to Houston to kick off the famous Livestock Show and Rodeo.

"The cinnamon toast recipe was developed by Steve's mom. She felt if she could not get her busy family to stop and eat breakfast, she could at least hand them a piece of toast that had a little better food value. Our guests love it with a big mug of milk.

"Steve's Skillet-Lickin' Omelets are his version of a farmer's omelet. He perfected the art while in the army working in the snack bar of the general's command building in Heidelberg, Germany."

Beer Bread

Yields 1 loaf

It's hard to believe that something as simple as this beer bread is so delicious. No waiting for the yeast to rise and no tedious kneading is involved, yet you end up with a loaf of "homemade" bread. It is really great toasted; and served with Fayetteville honey and assorted jams and jellies, it is positively a breakfast treat. Guests at the Lickskillet Inn often leave this friendly dining room with a "doggy bag" of beer bread, compliments of their hostess.

3 cups Martha White's self-rising flour
3 tablespoons sugar
8 ounces beer (your favorite brand), room temperature

Mix ingredients. Spray loaf pan with Pam. Pour mixture into pan and bake in preheated oven at 375° for 40 minutes, or until brown. Cool before slicing.

Steve's Skillet-Lickin' Omelets

Prepare in advance to build omelets by:
Making a mess of hash-browned potatoes
Frying or microwaving bacon
Sautéing onions, bell pepper, and mushrooms
Dicing up tomatoes and black olives
Grating two or three kinds of cheese (Steve uses a mild cheddar and mozzarella)
Gently whipping yard eggs with 1 tablespoon cream per omelet (2 eggs per omelet)

Pour eggs into 275° skillet and let set. Add any or all of the above ingredients down the center of the eggs. Just as the eggs begin to bubble slightly, fold one side over the stuffings. Then lop the other side of the eggs over. For best results, use two flapjack flippers.

Turn skillet to 300° and allow omelet to brown, then gently flip over and brown other side.

Absolutely superb topped with sour cream.

Grandma Donaldson's Original Cinnamon Toast

Yields 10 to 12 slices

1 cup sugar
¾ stick butter
1 large yard egg, beaten
Cinnamon to taste
10 to 12 slices bread, white or whole wheat

Mix first 4 ingredients together and spread on bread. Place under broiler until brown and bubbling hot.

The Luther
Palacios

The axiom over the Luther Hotel's front desk reads, "He who enters here is a stranger but once." This is definitely the philosophy of Elsie and Charles Luther, owners of this grand old dame on Palacios Bay. It is their home and yours, for when you enter the Luther's doors, you are no longer a stranger in Palacios. Even Yankees agree, for the same loyal clientele from the freezing North and Canada keep coming back here. Many of these "snowbirds" have been returning for ten or fifteen years, and it's no wonder why. The Luthers have the old-fashioned charm and grace to make everyone feel at home.

The Hotel was originally built on East Bay in 1903 and referred to as the Old Palacios Hotel. In 1905, however, it was moved on skids to four acres of land a half-mile away to face Tres Palacios Bay in order to attract more of the tourist trade. It must have been quite an undertaking, since the chimneys and porches had to be torn down and the solid cypress three-story structure moved in three sections.

The Luthers purchased the hotel in 1938, and there are fifteen neatly kept guest rooms and twenty-four apartments, most of which are rented for three-month intervals. There is a very romantic penthouse on the third floor for a private weekend without worldly confusion and stress. It has a giant bathtub, contemporary furniture, a king-sized bed, and the only television other than the one in the lobby. The hotel roof is the penthouse porch, so you have two beautiful views of the bay, one on top of the world and the other from your penthouse window. No friends or children are allowed to share the penthouse so your privacy is assured.

If you get a little bored with solitude, you can join "the family" in the game room for bridge or canasta, watch a little TV in the lobby, or do some midnight fishing off the pier (trout fishing is good in the fall). If duck and goose hunting is your forte, you'll find the nice marshes around Collegeport accommodating. For good camaraderie, though, having coffee with the other guests on the Luther's first floor is a must. Such notables as Sam Rayburn, Clark Thompson and his wife Libby Moody Thompson, Lyndon Johnson, Mike Driscoll, and Jim Wright have found the conversation very stimulating.

If you must have air-conditioning, tell Mrs. Luther when you call. Some of the hotel rooms are air-conditioned, but with the bay breezes floating through large windows aided by ceiling fans, you really don't need it. The motel rooms are artificially cooled, but then you can't really enjoy that fresh clean air.

The Luthers will soon have a second penthouse ready for guests. Known as the "Studio Quarters," it will be located on the east side of the third floor. Remember that there's no restaurant, but you won't starve in Palacios, because there are eating places to be found. On the other hand, who'll have time to eat out, with goose gumbo or fried trout cooking on your own stove? And don't be surprised if the Luthers grace your table with flowers, fresh fruit, or good company. They are such dear people, and you'll want so much to be a part of their "family."

Mrs. Luther has graciously given us a part of herself by sharing some congressional recipes. For 25 years the Luthers sent the following recipes to the congressional chef with the Texas delegation when the United States Congress was in session. How's that for southern hospitality!

Escalloped Oysters

Serves 4

    2 stacks of saltine crackers
    ½ pint washed oysters
    Butter or margarine
    1 pint whipping cream

Hand-crumble crackers into medium round casserole to cover bottom and sides. Cracker lining should be 1 inch thick or slightly less. Place oysters in single layer over the crackers. Place thin slices of butter over the oysters, covering all of them. Pour whipping cream over the contents until they are thoroughly moistened. Hand-crumble crackers over this to completely cover oysters and butter to a depth of about an inch. Place thin slices of butter over crackers; add whipping cream until the crackers are moistened and a surplus of cream stands around edges and on top. Sprinkle with paprika. Bake uncovered in 350° oven for about 45 minutes or until brown and crispy. Must be served piping hot.

Crab Au Gratin

Serves 4

½ stick butter or margarine
1 medium onion, chopped
½ bell pepper, chopped
2 prongs from a stalk of celery, chopped
1 medium-sized clove garlic
½ cup Wondra flour
¾ cup milk
¼ pint whipping cream
Dash paprika
½ teaspoon salt
1 heaping tablespoon Cheez Whiz
1 medium jar of sliced pimento
½ pound lump crabmeat

Melt butter in medium skillet; sauté vegetables and garlic until tender. To make cream sauce, add flour and milk and cook to proper consistency. Then add whipping cream. Add the chopped, sautéed vegetables to cream sauce with a generous dash of paprika, and salt. Add Cheez Whiz and pimentos; stir in prepared lump crabmeat. Taste for proper seasoning; pour in round casserole; bake at 350° until bubbly. Serve *hot*.

Shrimp Gumbo

Serves 4

Even though the Luther Hotel does not have a restaurant, members of the Luthers' winter family often gather for evenings of shared food and games and the special camaraderie of the Luthers themselves. Even if you are not ready to become a member of the Luther family, you can get a true taste of their friendliness with Elsie Luther's shrimp gumbo.

1 medium onion, chopped
½ bell pepper, chopped
Garlic to taste
½ cup chopped celery
1 medium jar pimentos
½ stick butter or margarine
1 7-ounce jar chopped pimentos
1 cup cooked rice
2 dozen boiled shrimp
1 pinch red pepper
Salt and black pepper to taste

Sauté onion, bell pepper, garlic, celery, and pimentos in butter until tender. Add pimentos, rice, and shrimp. Stir until well-mixed and hot. Add red pepper, salt, and black pepper.

Note: Since there is no roux or filé, gumbo purists will call this just a shrimp and rice dish. Whatever you call it, this is a very tasty recipe. How about Shrimp Luther?

The Magnolias
Jefferson

The Magnolias has it all — 1867 southern charm, architectural beauty, stories of clandestine meetings, untimely death, and a resident ghost. The graceful Greek Revival home sits high above Broadway, proudly displaying its lovely white colonnade, wide gallery, and red brick walk. This house is the very embodiment of the southern ideals that prevailed in Jefferson long after the Yankees initiated Reconstruction. Now an integral part of historic Jefferson, the Magnolias is on the National Register of Historic Places, is a recipient of the Texas Historical Medallion, and has been featured in *Early Texas Homes* and on "PM Magazine."

When we think of southern hospitality, we associate it with the waxy white blossoms of magnolias. The Magnolias, named after the huge trees in the mansion's garden, was built by Jefferson's cofounder, Dan Nelson Alley. He constructed the home for his daughter, Victoria, to ensure that her dowry would be sufficient to attract a prominent husband.

Victoria accomplished her father's desire and married a Confederate veteran and famed attorney, M. L. Crawford. Their life together was tragic, however; all three of her children — Love, Lucy, and Vic — died in infancy. Victoria died at age twenty-two giving birth to Vic. The Magnolias then went to the Crawford family, since Victoria's last child outlived her by twenty days.

Alley was proud of his heritage as a southerner, and history has it that he hated Yankee arrogance so much that he dismantled forty-five vacant houses and burned the lumber to keep scallywag and carpetbagger "riffraff" out of Jefferson. Of course, Alley spared the home he built for his Victoria.

It was in keeping with the era that the Magnolias was a secret meeting place for southern sympathizers (the White Committee) who wished to hold Jefferson together until citizens could regain control from Reconstructionists. A lookout would warn the faction of approaching Union soldiers. The Knights of the Rising Sun, of which W. L. Crawford

(Victoria's brother-in-law) was a member, also met here. This was a radical group known to have broken into the Jefferson city jail in 1868 and killed three back freedmen and one white man. At the Magnolias be sure to see the secret passageway to the attic, a small doorway camouflaged as a gun cabinet.

Victoria's husband, M. L. Crawford, was also a history-maker, playing a leading role in the legal proceedings for Jefferson's "crime of the century." Crawford was defense attorney for Abraham Rothschild, son of the diamond merchant of Cincinnati, who was accused of murdering "Diamond Bessie" Moore, his young pregnant bride. After seven years of trials and appeals, Rothschild was acquitted.

The one-and-a-half-story mansion has had thirty-five owners in 116 years, so it would be safe to conclude that there are probably many skeletons in the closet. There was one resident ghost, and whether he still resides in the Magnolias remains to be seen. The first report of the ghost was 10 years ago by one of the owners of the mansion, V. H. Hackney, former Jefferson mayor and retired chairman of Marshall National Bank. Mr. Hackney had invited a preacher and his wife to use the front drawing room for the weekend. Early the morning after the first night, the couple left in haste, saying they had heard doors closing, mysterious ghostly footsteps, and strange voices all night. Since then, the same phenomenon has been experienced by others. In fact, these strange events have been recorded on a tape recorder. It was later discovered that one owner of the mansion, Solomon A. Spellings, a Civil War veteran, committed suicide in the front drawing room because of failing health. Spellings' great-grandson, Jefferson resident Lyle Spellings, says his parents often reported that Solomon made his presence known to them in the house. Reports are that Hackney asked an Episcopal priest to come and bless the room, thus supposedly exorcising it.

With each owner, the Magnolias has taken on added charm. The A. W. Underhills and Mr. and Mrs. James R. Cornelius, Jr., jointly completed a major restoration fifteen years ago. Then Mr. and Mrs. Hackney continued the rejuvenation to the tune of $80,000. Since then, there has been some remodeling of the second level and repair work to the piers, sills, and porches. The new owners, Ken and Cheryl Kuesel, have added touches of their own, and innkeeper Cindy Evans is a hostess in the true southern tradition. Now a bed and breakfast, the Magnolias has two very comfortable private guest rooms with private baths (and yes, claw-footed Victorian tubs await you). An alcove and sitting area separates the two rooms, but this area can double as a third sleeping space for a third couple or a child. (Children must be at least twelve years old, which is certainly understandable considering the collection of antiques housed here.)

Ask Cindy to point out all the antique treasures, among them the Austrian-style Maria Theresa–pattern dining-room chandelier, the 1860 English tea set, and the 140-year-old Socttish grandfather clock encased in hand-carved mahogany eight and a half feet tall. Also note the painting of Victoria and a second of her husband and brother grandly altered, in Confederate uniform.

Once you've eaten Cindy's great breakfast, give yourself plenty of time to soak up local history. This old East Texas riverport has eighty-eight historical markers to its credit, including the 150-year-old Excelsior House, numerous restored homes, the McGarity saloon, and a lavish railroad car that belonged to railroad tycoon Jay Gould. Be sure to visit the 140-year-old Oakwood Cemetery, the Italian villa–style House of the Seasons, and the Freeman Plantation.

As for architecture, the wonderfully designed Magnolias has certainly deserved its place in the Historic American Buildings Survey of Architecture. In fact, a previous owner tells a wonderful story concerning the interest the structure has created. Recently, after a Shreveport honeymoon couple checked into the Magnolias, "a somewhat long-faced bride was seen reposed on the wide gallery of the back porch." Curiosity getting the better of the proprietor, he asked, "Pardon me, but . . . uh . . . where is your husband?" "He's in your attic," she replied in dismay. "He's an architect and had to see how the house was constructed — first!"

The magnetism of this lovely southern belle persists as a stately reminder of a romantic time lost forever but somehow forever present.

Quiche Lorraine

Yields 1 8-inch pie

Pastry
2 cups flour
½ cup Wesson oil
¼ cup milk
Pinch salt

Custard
1 cup whipping cream
4 egg yolks
Pinch salt
Pinch nutmeg
Pinch cayenne

Filling
6 to 8 slices bacon
8 ounces mozzarella cheese

Blend pastry ingredients together and then blend custard ingredients together. Fry bacon and drain on paper towels. Slice mozzarella and fill pastry (or individual pastry cups) with bacon and cheese. Pour on custard.

Bake in preheated oven at 375° for 35 to 45 minutes. Allow to rest 5 minutes before serving.

Bran Muffins

Yields 3 to 4 dozen

10 ounces raisin bran
5 cups flour
3 cups sugar
3 teaspoons baking soda
2 teaspoons salt
1 quart buttermilk
1 cup cooking oil
4 eggs, beaten

Mix dry ingredients in large bowl. Add liquids. Bake in muffin tins 15 to 20 minutes at 400°.

Batter will keep in refrigerator up to 6 weeks. Aging seems to improve the flavor.

Mansion
on Turtle
Creek
Dallas

If you ever find yourself with the duty of entertaining a king, an heiress, or a movie star but don't know where to take him or her, the Mansion on Turtle Creek is your answer. Owned by oil heiress Caroline Hunt Schoellkopf, daughter of H. L. Hunt, this luxurious hotel and restaurant is the stomping ground of the elitest of the elite. In fact, personages such as Ralph Lauren, Givency, Saudi princes, the queen of Thailand, the king of Norway, and Martha Graham have entered its front doors. And posh it is, with custom furniture, custom rugs, custom everything. Your every wish is their command; your every dream is fulfilled.

The mansion was originally the elegant Spanish-style residence of cotton trader Sheppard King. The family purchased the four and a half acres in 1908 from the Armstrongs, who subdivided large tracts of land to create the affluent Highland Park neighborhood near the Dallas downtown business district. King and his wife, in fact, built the third mansion of many in 1908. Then, in 1923, the old mansion was demolished to make room for their sixteenth-century Italian-style villa, which took two years to construct. The plans for this showplace were finalized only after the Kings and their architect, J. Allen Boyle, spent two years in Europe collecting ideas. They decided on a style influenced by both Italian and Spanish architecture, with stucco archways, wrought-iron trim, carved woodwork and fireplaces, and marble columns and floors. The result was magnificent, and the beauty remains to be admired today. In 1935 the Kings tired of the old and went with something new; they sold the mansion to Freeman Burford and his wife Carolyn Skelly.

In the 1940s it ceased to be a residence and was converted to offices for various businesses. With a restaurant in mind, however, Rosewood Hotels, Inc., a Hunt-owned corporation, purchased the home and began

115

extensive repairs. In August 1980 the classy restaurant opened to the public amid rave reviews of the cuisine, and the positive comments have been coming ever since.

With Avner Samuel as executive chef, they will probably keep coming. The recipient of the 1980 Food Parade Award of Israel and a native of that country with dual citizenship in France, Chef Avner received his education from the Tadmor School of Culinary Arts, Jerusalem, and La Varenne School of Culinary Arts, Paris. He has worked as executive *sous-chef* at the Boca Raton Hotel and Club in Boca Raton, Florida, and as chef at the Plaza Jerusalem Hotel in Israel.

So with international cuisine and international surroundings, another chic Texas restaurant was born. The refurbishing kept the overall European motif intact, and craftsmen worked to preserve such original details as the sixteenth-century German mantel that is now in the dining room, as well as a set of stained-glass windows that depicts the British barons signing the Magna Carta. (Mrs. King was a descendant of King Edward III of England.) Inside the foyer, a grand staircase that ascends two floors and features a wrought-iron railing with a coat-of-arms is also original. Rosewood Hotels, Inc., did their share, too, by adding such extras as a magnificent ceiling. The architect, sparing no expense, hired six craftsmen who spent two months installing 2,400 separate pieces of enameled and inlaid wood to make a breathtaking ceiling. The entire 10,000-square-foot, three-level mansion was completely converted into a restaurant and bar with smaller, private dining and meeting rooms off the main dining room, one of which is the Pavilion, the largest function room. Accommodating up to 200 persons, the Pavilion is decorated with trellised and mirrored ceilings, a champagne, green, yellow, and salmon color scheme, and elegant crystal chandeliers. The Promenade, where breakfast is served, has arched windows that overlook the lushly landscaped courtyard.

If this weren't enough, in April 1981 a 143-room, 9-story hotel was added on the premises, including 14 suites and a swimming pool. The cost of the entire project was approximately $21 million, with $145,000 spent on each unit. The 2 Terrace suites are on the top floor and embrace a spacious 1,250 square feet each. Each includes a huge bedroom, a large bath and separate shower, a living and dining room, a guest powder room, a fully equipped kitchen and bar, and a gorgeous terrace with a spectacular view of the Dallas skyline. Every room, however, whether it be a suite or a smaller 450-square-foot guest room, is nothing short of sensational, appointed with museum-quality art, custom-designed rugs from Portugal and the Orient, and specially designed moldings cast individually for each room.

116

Oh, and be sure to note the English Chippendale breakfront filled with a beautiful collection of Chinese porcelains and one original jardiniere by Paxton. Every three days, the jardiniere is replenished with thirty dozen fresh gladiolus flown in from Holland. How's that for class!

Pumpkin Linguini with Lobster and Sun-Dried Tomatoes

Serves 2

The owner of the Mansion on Turtle Creek, Caroline Schoellkopf, is convinced that pumpkins are more than silly jack-o'-lanterns. These hefty melons are rich in vitamins and minerals, and even their seeds are quite tasty. Nutritious, economical, delicious, and relatively low in calories, pumpkins are the perfect food. For a unique pumpkin delicacy, try the Mansion's linguini, but don't wait until Halloween.

½ cup semolina flour
1 teaspoon olive oil
2 eggs
2 tablespoons pumpkin puree
Salt
1 lobster (1 ¼ pounds)
Court bouillon
Clarified butter
Pepper
3 ounces lobster sauce
2 sun-dried tomatoes, cut into strips

Combine the flour, olive oil, eggs, pumpkin puree, and salt to taste in a food processor and process until dough forms. Remove and wrap in plastic wrap. Place in refrigerator and let rest 2 hours.

Cook lobster in boiling Court bouillon for 10 minutes. Remove meat from shell and cut into strips.

Work pumpkin dough through a pasta machine and cut into linguini. Cook in boiling salted water for 2 minutes. Place in the middle of a hot plate.

Sauté lobster in a hot pan with clarified butter. Add salt, pepper, and lobster sauce. Pour over linguini. Garnish with the sun-dried tomatoes and serve hot.

Tortilla Soup

Yields 12 large servings (1½ gallons)

4 cups onion puree
6 cloves garlic
64 ounces tomato puree
½ ounce cumin seed, crushed
2 bay leaves
1 sprig epasote (Spanish spelling is *ipazote*; a dry spice like parsley purchased in a Mexican food store)
1 dash crushed red pepper
2 corn tortillas, chopped
1 gallon chicken stock
Corn oil
Chicken pieces
Avocado pieces (¼ avocado per serving is ample)
Cheddar cheese

In a Swiss kettle, sauté onion puree and garlic until transparent. Add tomato puree, spices, and tortillas. Add chicken stock, taste for seasoning, and cook slowly for 1 hour. This will make the base for the soup. After this has cooked for 1 hour, place in a food processor and puree. Strain the soup to remove all large particles so that only the clear broth will remain. Reheat broth to very hot, or the garnishes will cause it to cool. (Garnishes should also be at room temperature for this reason.) Garnish the broth with chicken pieces, avocado pieces, and strips of tortillas sautéed in corn oil. Serve in bowls and garnish with cheddar cheese.

Sea Scallop Salad with Melon and Soya Vinegar

Serves 4

12 ounces sea scallops
20 endive leaves
1 apple
16 melon balls
3 bunches watercress
2 tablespoons olive oil
Salt and pepper
2 teaspoons toasted coconut

Sauce
¼ cup raspberry vinegar
2 tablespoons soya sauce
¼ cup olive oil
1 teaspoon whole-grain mustard
Salt and pepper

Slice the sea scallops in half. Cut the endive into 1-inch slices. Slice the apple with its skin into ½-inch strips and keep in cold water with 1 drop of lemon juice.

Mix the melon balls, apple, endive, and watercress. Cover and keep in refrigerator.

In a small mixing bowl, combine all ingredients for the sauce and stir for a few minutes. Store in refrigerator.

In a medium sauté pan over high heat, cook sea scallops in the olive oil until medium rare. Add salt and pepper to taste. Remove from heat, and strain the liquid.

Place the sea scallops over the lettuce. Pour over the sauce and garnish each plate with ½ teaspoon of toasted coconut.

Marriott's Hotel Galvez
Galveston

The Hotel Galvez, which opened on June 10, 1911, marked a new beginning for the city of Galveston. It rose from the total devastation of the 1900 killer hurricane, known as the "Great Storm." When the winds calmed and the seas subsided, 6,000 people had been killed and the beachside resort was flattened. But the heads of Galvestonians were "bloodied but unbowed," and reconstruction began as soon as the debris could be cleared. To encourage a new beginning, a group of prominent citizens decided to build a luxurious new hotel to draw tourists back to the island. They decided to name this grand hotel after count Bernardo de Galvez, also the namesake of the city, who was Spanish viceroy to Mexico when Galveston was part of Mexico.

The count was an enlightened leader who introduced numerous reforms and even befriended American revolutionists in the early 1800s. Galvez was a man of action, whose motto on his coat of arms reads, "Yo Solo," meaning "I alone," a philosophy that the city of Galveston adopted officially.

And so the hotel was named, and Hotel Galvez was born. Soon vacationers began to come back to this "Atlantic City of the South," a few at first and then droves. Wealthy families began arriving for the summer by train or steamer from New York, their servants taking smaller rooms across from their employers, who faced the Gulf. With them came new life to the Galveston that was almost a victim of the very thing it loved — the sea.

Among those who have signed the register are the Dorsey brothers, Paul Whiteman, Frank Sinatra, and Presidents Eisenhower, Nixon, and Franklin D. Roosevelt, the latter using the hotel as a temporary White House during his Galveston fishing trips. Pinup girl Alice Faye married bandleader Phil Harris in one of the suites here. Through the years the famous came and went, with Galveston slowly gaining back the prosperity it had lost and Hotel Galvez acquiring the title "Queen of the Gulf."

Queenly she was, with her Spanish mission–style exterior, the continuous row of massive interior arches, and her royal porte cochere entrance with its "Yo Solo" emblem commanding the respect of all who entered her doors. A large oil portrait of Count Galvez has always hung in the lobby, a fitting place for a man who had visionary plans for his favorite city. The Galvez has continued to reign graciously through decades. She has stood firm in spite of one hurricane after another, even during the recent major hurricane Alicia, a massive testimony to human conquest over the forces of nature.

In 1978 the Hotel Galvez closed, but the pause in its service was only temporary. The new owner, noted heart surgeon Dr. Denton Cooley, purchased the hotel that year because it reminded him of his childhood. Not only had his parents spent their wedding night there, but he had vacationed there frequently while he was a child and a medical student. Shortly after purchasing the hotel, he sold half his interest to Archie Bennett, Jr., of the Mariner Corporation. Together they decided to restore the Galvez and acquire a Marriott franchise. Thus began the $13 million dollar renovation, which lasted two years. Before it was all over, original elaborately carved woodwork was discovered behind false walls and ceilings; seventy-year-old doors were restored; and Peacock Alley, the hotel's promenade, once again came to life with wicker, ceiling fans, plants, and red patterned chairs and sofas. A pool was also added, along with a sauna, a whirlpool, and a game arcade. All and all, the entire ground floor has been refurbished to resemble the ground floor of 1911. In contrast, the upper floors are typically Marriott.

The Galvez dining room offers fresh seafood fare, including Seafood St. Jacques (a combination crabmeat, shrimp, and scallop dish), shrimp creole, and gumbo. It also serves a luncheon buffet that draws local regulars. Tim Kennedy, the food and beverage director, recommends the chef's special of the month, which usually provides a hearty helping of meat and seafood. Tim says his people strive to create dishes "indicative of the Galveston taste," as are the recipes that follow. The food here is indeed prepared and presented with the local resident in mind. Even the menu is in a photo album style, with the history and pictures of the city. (Be sure to ask to see the enlarged photos of turn-of-the-century Galveston that hang in the meeting rooms.)

A word of advice: when visiting Galveston, give yourself plenty of time to see all the sights. There is at least a week's worth of things to do.

Bacon-Wrapped Scallops

This simple, delightful hors d'oeuvre from the "Queen of the Gulf" can be assembled well in advance and stored in the refrigerator. Just prepare a lot, for they will disappear like magic. All you need is scallops, bacon, and a little butter for a real party favorite.

Determine the number of sea scallops required. The larger ones are best. For each 2 scallops, use 1 slice of bacon. Blanch bacon until it is half done, and cut in half across. Wrap scallop with one-half slice of bacon. Spear with a toothpick. Place scallops on an oiled pan. Baste scallops with butter. Bake in preheated oven at 350° for 10 to 15 minutes or until scallops and bacon are done.

Shrimp Creole

Serves 10

2 pounds bacon, diced into ¼-inch pieces
2 large yellow onions, diced into ½-inch pieces
3 large green bell peppers, diced into ½-inch pieces
1 bunch celery, diced into ½-inch pieces
1 No. 10 can (12½ cups) tomato puree
1 46-ounce can tomato juice
1 pint water
3 bay leaves
Salt and pepper
5 pounds shrimp, peeled and deveined (if frozen, thaw)
1 pound cooked rice

Sauté bacon until crisp. *Do not* drain. Add vegetables and sauté until soft. Add puree, juice, water, and spices. Simmer for 1½ hours. Salt and pepper to taste. Add shrimp and cook until shrimp are done (about 10 to 12 minutes). Serve over bed of rice.

French Onion Soup Au Gratin

Yields 1 gallon

1 gallon rich beef stock (made with bouillon; can substitute beef bouillon if necessary, but reduce salt)
3 pounds yellow onions (peeled weight)
¼ pound butter or margarine
1 pint burgundy wine
2 ounces Parmesan cheese, grated
¼ cup red wine vinegar
Salt and pepper to taste
1 slice bread per serving
1 slice (1 ounce) provolone cheese per serving

Bring beef stock to a boil. While stock is coming to a boil, peel and slice onions approximately ⅛ inch thick.

Melt butter in a large pan, add all the onions, and sauté until a dark golden brown, stirring constantly.

When onions are done, pour wine over them to deglaze pan.

Slowly add grated Parmesan to beef stock, stirring constantly.

When cheese has melted, add onions and red wine vinegar to stock. Simmer for 15 minutes. Salt and pepper to taste.

At service, cut bread into round croutons, spread with butter, sprinkle with Parmesan cheese, and toast. Float crouton on each serving of soup. Place 1 slice of provolone cheese on top of crouton and bake in 350° oven until cheese has melted and has a light golden crust, approximately 5 to 7 minutes.

The
Melrose
Dallas

Cemeteries and subdivisions have a tendency to sound alike, which is perhaps because you own your plot of ground in both. But Dallas's Oak Lawn is not for final interment, just one of the oldest neighborhoods in the city. Nor was this particular section of Dallas named by a slick real estate developer, but by a Civil War veteran, Colonel George Mellersh. Mellersh was so impressed by the magnificent oaks on his property that he christened his home in their honor, and the name has endured since 1876.

The Colonel's home later fell into ruins, and the Burgher family developed the property, but even the Burgher home had to go when the Melrose grew to dominate Oak Lawn in 1924. Back in the 1920s, apartment hotels were the rage among many of the wealthy — sort of precursors of modern high-rise condos — and the Melrose was one of Texas's most elegant and exclusive examples of this trend. Each guest room had an outside exposure, and one hundred of them included kitchens. The facade of the Melrose is unimpressive by modern standards, with its red brick and limited ornamentation, but in the twenties the hotel was considered posh indeed.

In spite of a remodeling in the 1950s and its faithful permanent residents, the Melrose seemed destined for the hard times that befall so many hotels past their prime. However, in 1981 Banyan Realty Corporation closed the old Melrose and with careful renovation has created a small, premier hotel with an abundance of old-world elegance.

Rooms are large and spacious and feature lovely appointments. (The kitchens are gone.) The lobby, with its forest green and white decor, is exquisite and formal, adorned by handsome antiques. You would never dream of raising your voice in the Melrose lobby. However, for gaiety and good camaraderie, one of the most charming bars in Dallas is the Melrose's Library. The walls are actually lined with books, creating an intimate atmosphere.

The beautiful Garden Court, with its Art Deco entry and crisp black, white, and dark green colors, sets the tone of casual elegance. Natural light from the unadorned windows bathes the Court at breakfast and lunch. At dinner, subdued lighting creates a more formal atmosphere. At every meal, gleaming silver and heavy white tablecloths add to the charm, as excellent food and impeccable service complete the perfection of the Melrose.

Cranberry Nut Cake

Yields 2 loaves

2 cups fresh cranberries, coarsely ground
2 cups nuts, chopped
2 tablespoons orange peel, grated
4 cups all-purpose flour
2 cups sugar
3 teaspoons baking powder
2 teaspoons salt
1 teaspoon baking soda
6 tablespoons shortening or butter
1½ cups orange juice
2 eggs, well beaten

Combine cranberries, nuts, and orange peel. Set aside. Mix dry ingredients in large mixing bowl. Cut in shortening. Stir in orange juice and eggs. Fold in cranberry mixture. Spoon into 2 greased and floured loaf pans. Bake at 350° for 60 minutes or until wooden pick inserted in the center comes out clean. Cool 15 minutes.

The Menger

San Antonio

San Antonio is fortunate to have four great historic hotels, all of which have been restored in a grand manner. Yet, as with all hotels of the past, each is special in its own way. The Gunter has its Swiss influence now, the Crockett its ultramodern interior, and the St. Anthony its elegance, yet each has a distinct and separate ambience. The oldest of the four is the marvelous Menger, dating back to William and Mary Menger's two-story 1859 building.

Lots of changes have taken place since 1859 at one of Texas's most famous hotels. A motor hotel has been attached and a swimming pool added to the patio, and you have to wander way down the lobby to admire the beautiful rotunda with its marble columns and art masterpieces. But the Menger has retained some of its old-fashioned ambience with a number of rooms furnished in magnificent antiques.

The Menger probably boasts more historical markers than any of Texas's other hotels. Sidney Lanier, the famous poet, lived in the Menger for a while, and Captain Richard King of the fabled King Ranch died here in 1885. Funeral services were held in the hotel.

In 1887 the Menger Bar was added, and this replica of the taproom in the English House of Lords has remained almost unchanged. Here O. Henry dreamed and wrote many of his stories with their famous ironic endings. Here Teddy Roosevelt recruited many of his Rough Riders for the Spanish-American War, and Teddy's pictures hang on the dark paneled walls.

All of the great generals of the Civil War were guests at the Menger — when they were fighting Indians instead of each other. World War I's "Blackjack" Pershing was another distinguished military figure who signed the register. Judge Roy Bean's beloved Lillie Langtry and the immortal Sarah Bernhardt added to the glorious past of this San Antonio heritage hotel, which stands next to the Alamo. It is amazing that the Menger has survived the onslaught of progress and remains one of the best hotels in the Southwest.

Mr. Abbott's Cheese Soup

Serves 6 to 8

Mr. Art Abbott has been the Menger's general manager for quite a number of years, and his cheese soup is on the menu in the Patio Room and in Menger Coffee Shop as well. That should give you a good idea of how popular it is with the Menger's guests. It is a shame that Teddy Roosevelt never tasted it, for his famous "Bully!" would have resounded throughout the historic Menger.

1 cup carrots, finely diced
1 cup celery, finely diced
½ cup onions, finely diced
3 tablespoons butter
3 tablespoons flour
½ tablespoon salt
1 teaspoon All 'n One seasoning or allspice
2 cups milk
1 quart chicken broth
4 ounces American cheese, diced

Sauté carrots, celery, onions, and butter in heavy saucepan over low heat until vegetables are soft. Do not scorch. Add flour, salt, and seasoning, and stir well. Blend in milk, broth, and cheese. Stir until cheese melts.

If too thick, add more milk or broth. Can be reheated.

Menger Hotel Spinach Pudding

Serves 12

If you think you have cooked spinach in every conceivable way, here is something different from the Menger — spinach cooked in a towel. Yes, in a towel. Don't use one of your designer kitchen towels to cook this dish, for the spinach may stain it forever and ever. Just use a plain old cuptowel that can always be your "spinach pudding towel."

3 cups cooked spinach, well drained
½ small onion
½ green pepper
1½ cloves garlic
4 eggs
1 teaspoon salt
¼ teaspoon pepper
Dash nutmeg
2 cups bread crumbs (no crust), finely ground
½ cup butter, softened

Put spinach, onion, green pepper, and garlic through grinder, using fine blade. Add eggs and seasonings, mixing well. Mix in 1½ cups of the crumbs.

Take a clean dishtowel and spread the butter onto it, forming a 9- to 10-inch square. Sprinkle with remaining bread crumbs. Drop spinach mixture in center and form a roll about 1½ inches thick. Wrap cloth loosely around roll. Tie ends and middle securely with string. Steam 20 minutes.

Mo-Ranch
Mountain Home

It is always entertaining to discover how Texas millionaires acquired their wealth. Even if it was with oil and cattle, it is fascinating to see what they did with their money. Fortunately, a great number of tycoons are anxious to leave behind some form of memorial that will earn them words of praise for their benevolence.

Dan Moran, president of Continental Oil Company, did not necessarily start Mo-Ranch with the idea of sharing it with the public. This fabled ranch was begun back during the Depression years, when about the only building going on anywhere was by the Civilian Conservation Corps. But Moran had no financial problems, and his huge ranch became a retreat for his family and friends.

Moran turned more than 6,000 acres of limestone, cedar, and mesquite overlooking the beautiful Guadalupe River into a ranch that even the Ewings of Southfork would envy. Even though the oil mogul spared no expense with his project, he did use tons of Conoco pipe throughout the buildings for supports. In the Great Hall, those pillars that look like giant cedar trunks are actually oil pipelines painted and curved to resemble cedar trunks. Also, a 290-foot pipe bridge spans a gorge with a fabulous view of the Hill Country.

Mo-Ranch has every type of guest accommodation imaginable. The Manor House and Guest Lodge offer a homey atmosphere, yet their architecture is reminiscent of castles in Spain. Winter must have been Moran's favorite time of year in the Hill Country, for massive fireplaces dominate the building. In the Guest Lodge the fireplace is aglow with rough-cut quartzite, amethyst, malachite, agate, and geodes — all Texas stones, of course. The Lodge's gleaming floor consists of crosscut slices of cedar bordered with Mexican tile.

For guests who prefer the convenience of a motel, there is the unit called Pheasant Run. Student and youth groups usually fill to capacity the two dormitories that can sleep 200 visitors. There are even eight apartments here at Mo-Ranch for those planning a longer visit. If camping is the way you enjoy a vacation, Mo-Ranch provides a top-drawer campground with grills, tables, electricity, and showers.

All guests at this unique ranch are free to use every recreational facility, and that includes a sparkling swimming pool; tennis, volleyball, and basketball courts; hiking trails; canoes; indoor games for rainy days (which are few in the Hill Country); and dining at the cafeteria-style Chow Hall.

Moran was not the original owner of Mo-Ranch, but it was his millions that created this famous Texas resort. The property of the Synod of Red River Presbyterian Church since 1949, the estate now serves as a church conference center. When the Presbyterians are busy elsewhere, Mo-Ranch is open to the public. Naturally, family reunions have found the perfect setting here in the Hill Country.

Canadian Cheese Soup

Serves 10

⅔ cup onion, finely chopped
1 cup bell pepper, finely chopped
1 cup celery, finely chopped
1 cup carrots, grated
½ cup butter
27½ ounces canned chicken broth
¼ cup flour
2 tablespoons cornstarch
¼ teaspoon paprika
1 teaspoon salt
¼ teaspoon white pepper
1½ teaspoons dried parsley flakes
4 cups whole milk
8 ounces sharp cheddar cheese, grated

Sauté onions, bell pepper, celery, and carrots in butter. Stir in chicken broth. Cover and simmer for 5 minutes. Combine dry ingredients and gradually stir in milk. Add milk mixture to vegetables and broth. Cover and simmer until thickened. Add cheese and heat on low until cheese is melted. Do not boil!

Mo-Ranch Biscuits

Yields 40 to 50 biscuits

This is a favorite recipe of a group of porcelain artists who spend a week at Mo-Ranch each fall.

Dissolve
1 package yeast in 1 cup warm water

Add
2 cups buttermilk
½ cup cooking oil
½ cup sugar
6 cups self-rising flour
½ teaspoon soda
1 teaspoon salt

Knead well. Add more flour if needed (about 7 cups to make a stiff dough). Store in airtight container in refrigerator for 12 hours before cooking. This will keep for weeks in refrigerator. Pinch off amount needed and roll on floured board. Bake at 400° for 15 minutes.

It needs to rise 1 hour before baking.

Hot Baked Fruit

Serves 8

1 pound pitted prunes
8 ounces dried apricots
1 13-ounce can pineapple chunks, undrained
1 1-pound can cherry pie filling
20 ounces water
¼ cup dry sherry
⅓ cup slivered almonds, toasted

Put prunes, apricots, and pineapple in a deep pan. Combine cherries, water, and sherry. Pour over fruit; mix well. Stir in almonds, cover, bake at 350° for 1½ hours. This freezes beautifully and refreezes.

Nutt
House
Granbury

If old-fashioned hot-water cornbread tickles your fancy or flatters your appetite, then a historic visit to the Nutt House in Granbury is for you. Many of the recipes used there are actual secrets cooked up in the late 1800s for passing drummers, famous actors and actresses performing at Granbury's majestic opera house, and a gunslinger or two. The history buff in you will love the town of Granbury, intact and prosperous but seemingly oblivious to the modern world. The place is teeming with medallions of historic places, with the entire town square placed on the national Register of Historic Places. In fact, there is not room here to name all the awards the square has won, among them the prestigious Lester Award for the preservation of a part of Texas history.

The Nutt House, however, has gained unending fame for its wonderful country "folk cooking." It's an art and certainly treated as such here in these hand-hewn Hood County stone walls. Former owner Mary Lou Watkins, great-granddaughter of the first Nutts, is solely responsible for not only preserving this authentic cuisine but also encouraging the restoration of the town. The new owner, Tony Dauphinot of Fort Worth, intends to continue with tradition; rest easy, because Mary Lou's cornbread is still on the menu. In fact, you can purchase the mix in the Nutt House gift shop, though Mary Lou has so graciously given the recipe to us here.

The history of the wonderful old hotel and restaurant began when blind brothers Jesse and Jacob Nutt, after donating acreage to help establish the Hood County seat at Granbury, decided to build the first store of Granbury. In 1866 a sixteen-foot by twelve-foot log house was constructed on the very site where the Nutt House stands today. In 1893 David, a younger brother, replaced the log store, using cypress and stone. It then became Granbury's combination store, hotel, and restaurant. Actually, David's wife was instrumental in getting the new structure built, after her husband continually invited transient stagecoach passengers to their home to sleep and eat. At any rate, the Nutt establishment became a favorite for residents and strangers alike, with much business resulting from the bustling train station located a few blocks away.

Today the Nutt House, which reopened in April 1970, still offers an abundance of local delights, including chicken and dumplings, meat loaf, ham, four vegetables in season, salads, relishes, buttermilk pie, cobbler, and of course the famous, world-renowned, scrumptious, unsurpassable hot-water cornbread.

You may want to stay a night and rest a spell in this little Texas haven. The people are friendly; life is easy; and the history there grabs you like a well-composed history book. At the Nutt House, accommodations have fourteen-foot ceilings and period furnishings in all nine rooms, with antique beds and dressers. Some have wicker furniture, which was so popular at the turn of the century. Wicker can also be found at the head of the stairs, where there's a reading parlor. If you like old documents, spend some time here with the wonderful old ledgers and receipt books full of jargon from a bygone era. (Take some time to go through the Nutt House scrapbook. You'll not only learn much about the hotel, but you'll also get a history lesson on Granbury.)

Five new rooms with baths and the Honeymoon Suite have been added in another building on the square. The latter is a beautifully decorated suite consisting of a bedroom with a double bed, one and a half baths, and a kitchen with eight tin-foot curve-topped windows. A weekend in the suite is a good way to leave the modern world behind.

Some famous names have been associated with Granbury over the years. In the late 1800s, Granbury had five saloons on the square. In 1870 John St. Helen, a young stranger with a limp, came to town in search of a bartending job. While working at one of the saloons, he became seriously ill, and it was thought he was dying. According to local sources, while on his supposed deathbed, St. Helen confessed that he was the infamous John Wilkes Booth. As soon as he recovered, he left town in haste and was never heard of again. Then some very incriminating evidence was found when the house where St. Helen had resided was moved. It seems a derringer like the one used to kill Lincoln was found wrapped in newspaper accounts of the assassination.

Other history-making characters had Granbury in common. For example, according to legend, Billy the Kid took violin lessons here while he was a "kid." Belle Starr hid here once, and Jesse James is allegedly buried in the Granbury Cemetery. As for other famous bones, Elizabeth Crockett, wife of Davy, is buried in the nearby Acton cemetery. Elizabeth moved to Granbury after Davy died at the Alamo, and as a result, there are still descendants of Davy here.

Go to Granbury, then, to soak up the local color and visit the Nutt House for some well-earned calories. The food is so good that the resident Presbyterians once advertised in the local paper that Sunday service was being changed to 9:30 A.M. to ensure that the congregation would be able to arrive for Sunday lunch at the Nutt House before the Baptists did.

Buttermilk Pie

Yields 1 9-inch pie

½ cup margarine
2 cups sugar
3 eggs
3 tablespoons flour
1 cup buttermilk
Dash nutmeg or vanilla or lemon extract
1 9-inch uncooked pie shell

Cream together margarine and sugar. Add eggs and flour into this mixture and beat until fluffy. Then fold in buttermilk and a dash of nutmeg or extract. (At the Nutt House, Madge and her people use nutmeg.) Pour into pie shell and bake 45 or 50 minutes at 350°.

Chicken Livers

Thaw frozen livers in water. With livers wet, roll in flour mixed with salt. (The proportions, of course, depend upon the size of your group and the heartiness of appetite.) Place in a shallow pan and brush with melted butter. Sprinkle with paprika and bake at 350° for about 20 minutes or until done. Madge cautions not to overbake, as this will make the livers hard.

Hot-Water Cornbread

Yields 2 dozen small round cakes

If there is any food more southern than grits, it would be hot-water cornbread. After all, what else do you eat with your turnip greens and potlikker? Long before the Civil War, slaves and slaveowners ate this economical bread with just about every meal.

When Mary Lou Watkins opened the Nutt House, this item was one of her smash hits. Since then, thousands of Yankees and Texans have succumbed to the delights of this really basic cornbread.

Madge Peters, the Nutt House manager, says, "These are often mistaken for hushpuppies, but they are really cornbread. We serve many thousands every week. Each piece is 'personally patted,' and the kitchen help says what they think about them couldn't be published." But there is no other way to make authentic hot-water cornbread than to "personally pat" each cake.

1 cup white cornmeal
1 cup yellow cornmeal
1 teaspoon salt
2 tablespoons bacon drippings
2 cups boiling water
½ teaspoon baking powder
2 tablespoons water
Cooking oil

Mix both cornmeals and salt. Add bacon drippings and boiling water into meal and stir. Set aside to cool (about 45 minutes to 1 hour).

After dough has cooled, work in baking powder dissolved in the 2 tablespoons of water. Pinch off a piece of dough and pat into a small round cake (Mary Lou used to say, "About the size of a duck egg"). Either fry the cakes immediately in deep fat hot enough to bubble freely over the bread (about 380°), or store them in the refrigerator on waxed paper for cooking a few hours later. Storing does not alter the flavor of the cakes in any way.

The cakes should have a crisp crust on the outside yet be soft on the inside. A little practice will give you the knack for this southern delicacy. When you spread on the butter, you'll agree with all of the Nutt House guests that this is *real* cornbread.

Sauerkraut Salad

Yields 10 servings

1 quart sauerkraut, drained
2 cups celery, diced
1 green pepper, diced
1 small can pimentos, chopped
2 cups sugar
½ cup wine vinegar

Combine all ingredients and let stand covered in the refrigerator 24 hours before serving.

House Dressing

Yields 5 cups

¼ cup soy sauce
4 tablespoons red wine vinegar
1 tablespoon ginger
¼ chopped onion
1 quart Kraft mayonnaise

Mix the first four ingredients together in the blender, then add mayonnaise.

The ginger gives this dressing a very distinct flavor and makes a good spread for roast sandwiches.

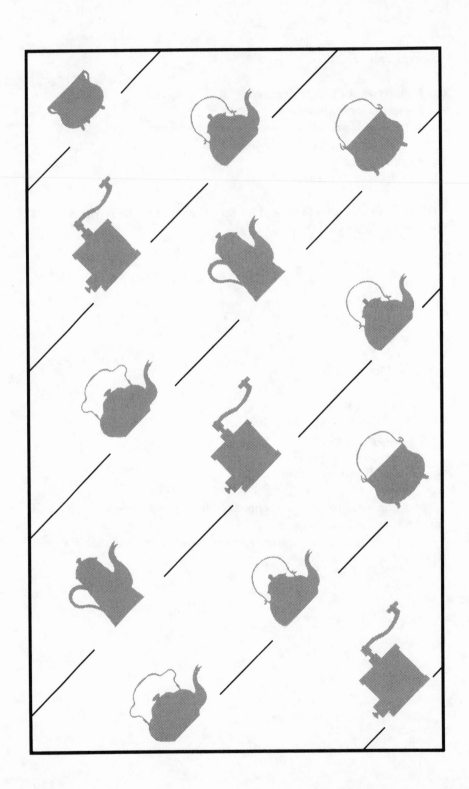

Hotel Paso del Norte
El Paso

The early 1900s were truly the era of the "grand hotels," and one of America's grandest ladies of them all was the Hotel Paso del Norte. Dallas may have had its Adolphus and San Antonio its Menger, but no other city could boast of a marble lobby crowned with a priceless Tiffany dome. This treasure arrived 'way out in the West Texas town of El Paso when Zach White opened the doors of his Paso del Norte in 1912. Zach certainly spared no expense with his construction, and El Paso's elite society added to the Paso del Norte's glitter and fame.

These were also the days in the border's turbulent history when the darling of Mexico's revolutionaries was Pancho Villa. The Rio Grande bridge between El Paso and Juárez carried a constant stream of refugees either fleeing Mexico or returning, depending on which dictator was in power. El Pasoans and members of the press cheered Villa to victory during the Battle of Juárez from the Paso del Norte's upper floors. Bullets nicked the hotel's walls, but their hero, Villa, won the battle.

At nearby Fort Bliss, an unknown officer would become famous when the United States became disenchanted with Pancho Villa and assigned "Blackjack" Pershing to track down the bandit. Villa was never apprehended, but Pershing went on to fame and glory in World War I.

Famous political figures have occupied the Paso del Norte's rooms. Presidents Obregón, Díaz, Taft, and Hoover signed the register, as did Richard Nixon as vice-president. A formal state luncheon for Lyndon Johnson and Díaz Ordaz was held under the Tiffany dome following the signing of the Chamizal Treaty in 1968.

Adding more glamor to this "showcase of the west" were Gloria Swanson, Will Rogers, Eleanor Roosevelt, The Great Caruso, Charles Lindbergh, and Amelia Earhart. Mystery writers Don Hamilton and Erle Stanley Gardner each used the hotel as the setting for a bestseller.

With the advent of chain motels on the interstate highway, the demise of the passenger trains, and the usual wear and tear of age, the Paso del Norte seemed destined to become another boarded-up and forgotten downtown hotel that had outlived its usefulness. When El Paso approached her four hundredth birthday, a group of business and civic organizations formed a project called "Renaissance 400." Their ambitious goal was to make the entire city of El Paso the "showplace of the west," and that included a complete restoration of the Paso del Norte as a hotel and the Cortez Hotel as an office building.

The Paso del Norte will have a new structure added, and with the renovation of the original hotel, 400 luxury rooms will be open by 1985. All it will take is about $40 million. This mammoth project is due to the foresight of Evern Wall, president of El Paso's electric company; Amfac Hotels, the firm that made the Adolphus a showplace, will handle the Paso del Norte's promising future. Wall anticipates "an Adolphus on the Rio Grande"; however, even the Adolphus with all of its priceless art objects cannot show them off under a Tiffany dome.

Spanish Avocado Bisque

Serves 8

This simple recipe is superb and a real favorite when a cold soup is the perfect way to start a meal. You do not even have to turn on the stove.

2 avocados (whole)
2 cups chicken broth
3 tablespoons lemon juice
¾ tablespoon salt
Dash cayenne
1 cup light cream
Toasted almonds, bacon bits, and diced tomatoes for garnish

Puree avocados with broth, lemon juice, and seasoning. Blend in cream. Cover and chill. Serve with garnishes.

Charcoal-Grilled Chicken with Garlic Puree

Serves 4

1 3-pound frying chicken
2 heads garlic
½ bottle red wine
2 to 3 sprigs fresh thyme or 1 teaspoon dried thyme
1 cup virgin olive oil
Salt and pepper to taste

Cut chicken into serving pieces; peel 8 to 10 cloves of garlic and chop them roughly. Marinate chicken in wine with chopped garlic and thyme for 2 to 4 hours in refrigerator.

Spread remaining cloves of garlic, with skins on, in a small baking dish in one layer and cover with olive oil. Sprinkle with salt and pepper and bake in preheated 300° oven for 1½ hours or until the garlic is completely soft. Puree garlic through a food mill when done. Discard skins and reserve puree.

About an hour before cooking chicken, remove it from refrigerator. Prepare a medium-low charcoal fire. When fire is ready, remove chicken from marinade, pat pieces dry, and salt and pepper them. Cook chicken on grill slowly for about 35 minutes, turning frequently. Chicken should be nicely browned but a bit rare and juicy. Spread garlic puree over chicken and heat in 375° oven for 5 minutes. Serve chicken on a platter with oven-roasted potatoes, garnished with watercress and lemon wedges.

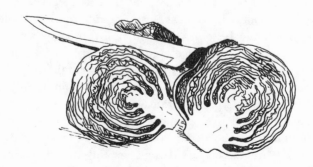

Rice Carlotta

Serves 8 to 10

Rice Carlotta is guaranteed to take a lot of time and just about every pot in the average kitchen. The good news is that you prepare it the day before, it is extremely delicious, and it is quite a conversation piece.

If this dish is representative of the Paso del Norte's Tiffany Restaurant, West Texans may be in for the finest gourmet food in the state.

This dessert must be refrigerated overnight, so plan accordingly.

1 cup golden raisins
½ cup peach brandy
1½ envelopes unflavored gelatin
½ cup long-grain white rice
5 cups milk
3 tablespoons unsalted butter
1½ teaspoons almond extract
1¼ cups sugar
6 egg yolks, room temperature
3 tablespoons peach preserves
1 cup heavy cream, chilled

In a small bowl, combine raisins with brandy; stir in gelatin and set aside to soften.

Bring 3 quarts of water to a boil and stir in rice. Cover and boil 5 minutes; remove from heat and let stand for 10 minutes. Drain rice.

In a large saucepan, bring 3½ cups of milk, butter, almond extract, and ½ cup sugar to a boil. Add rice, cover, and reduce heat to low. Simmer gently, stirring occasionally, for 1¼ hours, or until liquid has been absorbed and rice is very tender. Set aside and let cool completely.

Meanwhile, in a large bowl, beat egg yolks until thick and pale, about 5 minutes. Gradually beat in remaining ¾ cup sugar and continue beating until mixture is lemon-colored and falls from beater in a slowly dissolving ribbon. In a small saucepan, bring remaining 1½ cups of milk to a boil over high heat. Very slowly whisk boiling milk into egg yolk mixture in a thin stream. Transfer mixture to a heavy medium-sized saucepan and cook over low heat, stirring constantly, until custard thickens enough to coat a wooden spoon, about 10 minutes. Add raisin and brandy mixture and cook, stirring constantly, until gelatin is completely dissolved, about 1 minute longer. Stir in peach preserves; remove from heat and let custard cool completely.

Fold rice into cooked custard and refrigerate until custard is the consistency of stiffly whipped cream, about 1 hour; do not allow to set completely.

Meanwhile whip heavy cream until it forms stiff peaks. Gently fold whipped cream into rice custard.

Generously oil an 8-cup mold. Turn rice custard into mold, cover with waxed paper, and refrigerate overnight.

Before serving, run a wet knife around rim of mold, then dip mold into hot water for a few seconds. Unmold onto a round platter. Surround rice with peach preserves.

Is it worth the trouble? Absolutely!

Pfeiffer House
Bastrop

Bastrop has an abundance of historical markers, but it should come as no surprise, for after all, this is one of the oldest settlements in Texas. Back when Spain ruled Texas, a stop on the old San Antonio Road was located here, but named Mina. Famous travelers passed this way, including those early pioneers Uncle Billy Barton, Josiah Wilbarger, and Reuben Hornsby.

With all the upheaval in Texas politics, Mina swapped names with Bastrop a few times, but in 1837 Bastrop became the official town. One of the best friends the Republic of Texas ever had was baron Felipe Enrique Neri de Bastrop. This man with the impressive name had a vague background to go with it. Various historians have made him Prussian or French, but in the baron's will, he stated he was born in Holland.

Actually, where Bastrop was born is unimportant. The fact is that it was due to his influence that Governor António María Martínez reconsidered Moses Austin's request for colonization and in 1820 made one of the most fateful decisions in Mexican history. With the arrival of the Anglos, Mexico would only be a destructible obstacle in the path of America's "Manifest Destiny."

Bastrop continued to be a great friend to Stephen F. Austin and always sought legislation favorable to immigration. According to the Mexican system, Bastrop was paid with contributions from his constituents. Ironically, Texans were not as generous with their aid to their benefactor, and Bastrop died so destitute that contributions had to be solicited for his funeral. At least a city and county in the state and nation he befriended bear his name.

Bastrop is nestled among huge pine trees known as the "Lost Pines." These evergreens are a marooned stand of timber that was once part of the forests of east Texas. The Ice Age caused such flooding and erosion that these pines were isolated between the Gulf Coast and the Hill Country. Naturally, lumbering would become Bastrop's prime industry.

At the turn of the century, one of the major builders in this old town was J. R. Pfeiffer. His art and handicrafts can be seen in many of Bastrop's homes, but the Pfeiffer House is particularly charming. He built it in 1901 for his bride, Freda. Known as "Carpenter Gothic," the design was taken from pattern books, but Mr. Pfeiffer always added his own particular touches to his houses.

Papa and Freda filled their home with six little Pfeiffers, and one of their daughters, Marie Renick, recalls how very special Christmas was in this house:

> On Christmas Eve we had our traditional dinner. Mama always fixed a herring salad with a different ingredient for each petition in the Lord's Prayer. I never did like it, but I wish I had done herring salad for my children.

(Julia Watkins, Marie's older sister, recalls the seven ingredients as pickled herring, potatoes, apples, onions, salt, pepper, and vinegar. Lots of German families served this dish, but each was special to the different families.)

Marie continues with her memories of Christmas:

> Papa was always mysteriously called away after dinner, and then in a little while, the doors would slide open and we saw our beautiful tree decorated for the first time. It's amazing why those candles didn't burn down the house. Santa arrived, and we each had to make a Christmas speech learned especially for Santa.
>
> Somehow, we never connected Papa's leaving and Santa's arrival.

Papa and Freda would feel right at home if they came back to Pfeiffer House today. Marilyn White's touches have turned back the years. A grandfather clock marks the passing of the years in a formal Victorian parlor. The heavy sliding doors still close off the dining room where the Pfeiffers ate their herring salad.

Delightful bric-a-brac in every nook and cranny creates a perfect Victorian decor. Marvelous old lamps with their hand-painted shades are a special delight. Not every matched pair of shades was acquired at the same place at the same time, or at the same price. Marie Renick said that the house is furnished almost exactly like Mama's.

Different owners prior to the Whites have left their marks since Papa and Freda died. All the ceilings were sprayed in the tacky "sparkle" effect so popular in the 1960s. It is almost impossible to paint over, and Marilyn is racking her brain for economical methods to get rid of that un-Victorian glitter. Fortunately, Papa's beautiful handwork on the bullet-hole trim was left untouched, and his ornate entry and dining room china cabinet are still as handsome as the day he completed the house.

Marilyn offers three guest rooms for visitors anxious to enjoy the charm of this old town. Each is absolutely a Victorian dream, and with your room comes the Whites' gracious hospitality and breakfast. Who knows? Perhaps one Christmas Eve, herring salad will once again be a tradition.

The Pfeiffer-Whites' House Best Cookies

Yields 4 dozen

In addition to creating a little world of hospitality in this old home, Marilyn is an excellent cook. Awaiting every guest in his or her room is "a jar of these cookies along with a basket of fruit. Guests seem to really enjoy the 'homemade and old-fashioned taste,' and they are always a topic of conversation!"

1 cup flour
1 cup sugar
½ cup Crisco shortening
1 egg
1 tablespoon molasses
1 teaspoon cinnamon
1 teaspoon salt
1 teaspoon vanilla
¾ teaspoon baking soda
1 cup oatmeal
1 cup chocolate chips

Combine all ingredients. Bake at 350° for approximately 8 to 10 minutes. *Do not overcook.* Marilyn allows for exactly 9 minutes in her oven. Make certain that you check at 8 minutes. They will look almost under-cooked. Remove from oven when they are just turning tan on top, yet still soft.

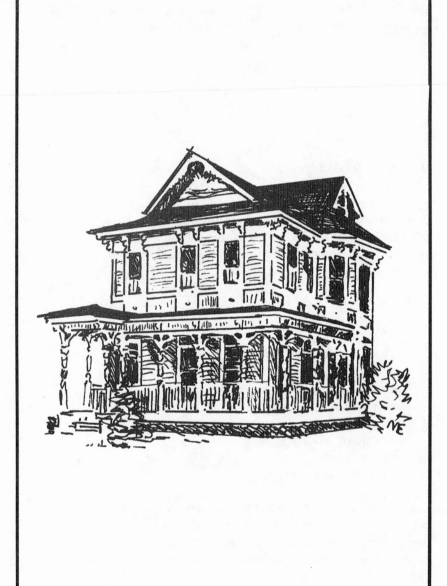

Pride
House
Jefferson

How would you like to wake up in a marvelous bedroom to a breakfast of exotic melons, croissants, poached pears, bran muffins with strawberry butter, a breakfast quiche, or perhaps a bread pudding with praline sauce? If this sounds like your idea of heaven, just go to Pride House in Jefferson and let Ruthmary Jordan pamper you.

Pride House is a gorgeous Victorian masterpiece complete with a cupola and widow's walk. White gingerbread trim and stained glass in every window add to its majesty. Ancient pecan trees shade the wide lawn, and an inviting swing makes an ideal spot from which to watch the tranquility of Jefferson in review.

Ruthmary and her daughter Sandy restored this old mansion and named it for Sandy's daughter, Pride Spaulding. Sandy and Pride have moved away, but Ruthmary continues to open her home for guests. You can stay in one of four lovely bedrooms, each with its own bath and telephone. Furnishings are not limited to one period but are a delightful blend of many eras. Wonderful pieces of antique wicker add charm to the spacious bedrooms.

A Victorian parlor with a cozy fireplace blazing on Jefferson's raw winter days beckons guests to visit and chat, and books and magazines are everywhere for browsing. One particularly outstanding feature of Pride House's decor is the handsome wallpaper border used on the walls. Ornate and funky, it adds a unique touch to the high walls.

In the rear of Pride House is a small white cottage called the "Dependency." In yesteryear when servants were dependents, they occupied quarters known as the dependency. Now, this little saltbox of a house can sleep seven guests comfortably and is often filled with families meeting for a weekend. A porch swing, an attic room, old kitchen paraphernalia, and eclectic furnishing make you yearn to be Pride House's "dependents."

Ruthmary brings her gourmet trays up to break the fast around 8 A.M. and arranges them in the gigantic armoire in the hallway. Guests can pick up their feasts at their leisure. You can have breakfast in bed or bask in the morning sun on the porch as you savor the delicacies of Pride House.

Gran Sally's Bread Pudding

Serves 6

Ruthmary refers to this old-time dessert as "a rich version of a Depression Era staple from my childhood."

1 dozen brown-and-serve rolls, cooked and dried
Approximately 1 cup whole milk
½ cup sugar
1 teaspoon vanilla
½ teaspoon nutmeg
½ teaspoon cinnamon
4 eggs, beaten

Crumble rolls in small pieces. Cover with milk. Add remaining ingredients and mix well. Grease baking dish with generous amount of butter or margarine and heat in oven until very hot. Then pour bread mixture into hot dish immediately and return to 350° oven to bake until a knife comes out clean, approximately 25 minutes. Pride House uses individual gelatin molds for baking dishes.

To serve: Spoon praline sauce in bottom of individual serving dishes. Place serving of pudding over the praline sauce and top with rich cream.

Praline Sauce
1 16-ounce box dark brown sugar
¾ cup cream
¼ cup Karo syrup, light or dark
2 tablespoons butter
¼ teaspoon vanilla

Mix sugar, cream, and syrup and boil 5 minutes. Add butter and vanilla. Cool and refrigerate.

Poached Pears

Serves 4 to 6

There is never anything ordinary about breakfast at the Pride House. Even if all you usually ever have is a piece of dry toast and a cup of coffee, there is no way you can resist the gourmet delectables that Ruthmary brings upstairs for her guests. After all, just how often do you get poached pears with a rich cream sauce to begin your day?

**1 package day-old bran muffins
1 package mincemeat
Orange juice for correcting consistency
Dash cloves, nutmeg, cinnamon
4 to 6 medium to large pears**

Core pears from the bottom, leaving stem end intact. Fill core with muffins, mincemeat, and spices that have been mixed in food processor. Bake covered about 30 minutes at 400°. Remove cover, cool, and refrigerate until needed. Pears can be frozen for lengthy storage.

Cream Sauce

Yields 4 cups

Ruthmary says she uses this sauce for several dishes, and it will keep refrigerated for about 5 days, so she makes large amounts.

**4 cups whole milk
1 cup sugar
¾ cup flour
4 eggs
2 teaspoons vanilla (Mexican strong vanilla preferred)**

Scald milk in double boiler. Mix sugar, flour, eggs, and vanilla at low speed in mixer. Add 2 cups hot milk to sugar mixture and continue to mix about 1 minute. Add sugar and milk mixture to remaining 2 cups of hot milk in double boiler. Stir constantly until desired thickness is reached. Strain. Cool and refrigerate to use as needed. Ruthmary prefers consistency of thick cream.

Prince
Solms
Inn
New Braunfels

In this age of television, Germans obviously no longer yearn for Valhalla; they just want to go to Texas. A delightful anecdote about German fascination with Texas and the West is told by Norbert Wilhelm, a naturalized American and ardent Texan. He says, "So many relatives and friends come to visit from Germany to see cowboys and Indians. The best I can do is take them to the Alabama-Coushatta Indian Reservation, and I've made so many trips, they should make *me* a member of the tribe."

Even a long time ago, before TV westerns, Germans wanted to be a part of Texas. In 1842 fourteen German noblemen founded a society for the colonization of Texas called the *Adelsverein*. Taken in by several con artists, the German aristocrats poured fortunes into their scheme only to go bankrupt by 1848. But Texas owes the *Adelsverein* a great debt, for one of their members, Prince Carl of Solms Braunfels, was responsible for founding one of the best tourist towns in the state.

The prince was not enchanted with Texas and tarried only a few months in New Braunfels. He did sort of set the tone of the community, however, when he threw a party that cost $25,000. Just think what a staggering sum that was in 1845! Talk about a whopper of a wurstfest! If the aristocratic prince were to visit his Texas namesake these days, he would never go back to the drafty old *schloss* in Germany. He would take up residence in the charming inn bearing his name, the Prince Solms.

This elegant little inn began its existence in 1899 with the unromantic name of the Comal Hotel. Built by one of the first immigrants, Christian Herry, it is considered one of Texas's architectural treasures. The present owners, Marge Crumbaker and Betty Mitchell, have added gorgeous antiques to every room, landscaped a delightful patio, and created three suites.

The guest rooms upstairs are named for their wallpaper: Rose, Magnolia, Peony, Penelope, and the enchanting Songbird. Then there is the Summerhouse and the Library with its stuffed and crammed bookshelves.

Down in the basement, a gourmet restaurant has been added named Wolfgang's Keller. (That cellar in English.) Victorian decor, soft candlelight, and the strains of beautiful music played on the grand piano by your host, Bill Knight, create the perfect setting for memorable evenings. Majestically approving of the whole arrangement is a huge oil painting of Wolfgang Mozart by Texas artist Emily Hocker. Even a prince would relish the menu.

Linguini with Clam and Shrimp Sauce

Serves 4

1 pound linguini, fresh if available
3 tablespoons clean cold pressed olive oil
3 tablespoons safflower oil
3 garlic cloves, finely minced
¾ cup fresh parsley, chopped
1 tablespoon fresh oregano (or ⅛ teaspoon dried)
1 cup minced clams with liquid
½ pound peeled raw shrimp chopped into ¼ -inch pieces

Cook linguini approximately 10 minutes in boiling water with a drop of olive oil. Check to make certain the pasta is *al dente*. Keep warm.

Heat olive oil and safflower oil in skillet. Add garlic. (Use more garlic if you really like garlic.) Cook over low heat for several minutes. Add parsley and oregano, clams with liquid, and chopped shrimp. Heat until good and hot and shrimp turns pink.

Serve immediately over hot linguini, and pass bowls of grated Parmesan cheese and dried red pepper flakes.

Chicken Piccata

Serves 4

When *Houston Post* columnist Marge Crumbaker was researching George Washington for a bicentennial project, she found that Chicken Piccata was the favorite dish of our first president. Amazingly, this old recipe was identical to the one used at Wolfgang's Keller. Part of the authenticity of Chicken Piccata is using Madeira wine, which Washington insisted was an absolute necessity.

4 8-ounce chicken breasts, skinned
Flour, salt, pepper, paprika
2 tablespoons clarified butter
1 tablespoon vegetable oil
2 tablespoons Spanish Madeira wine
Capers for garnish

Pound breasts with the flat side of a veal pounder. Dredge in flour seasoned with salt, pepper, and paprika. Heat butter and vegetable oil in skillet until very hot. Sauté chicken breasts 1 minute on each side. Remove and drain on paper towel. Pour off all but 2 tablespoons of oil and butter, and add 2 tablespoons of Madeira. Cook for a minute or so, scraping bottom of skillet. Place chicken breasts on plates and pour wine sauce over each breast. Garnish with a few capers on top of each portion.

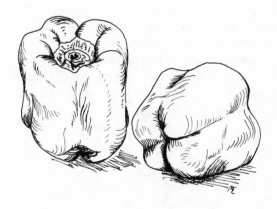

Wiener Schnitzel à la Wolfgang

Serves 4

Talented, debonair chef and host Bill Knight was a maestro of the keyboard long before becoming a maestro of Wolfgang's Keller's ovens. Here in the cellar of the Prince Solms you can enjoy Bill's expertise in the kitchen as well as his facility at the piano. Bill supervises the food purchases and the recipes, which are all carried out in first-class fashion by a wonderful lady named Sofía Díaz. As you are dining on great food, Bill will make your evening complete as he plays his enchanting renditions on the grand piano.

4 slices veal, 4 ounces each (use leg of veal, or better still, rib eye of veal)
1 teaspoon salt
1 cup flour
2 eggs, beaten
1 tablespoon water
Seasoned bread crumbs
4 tablespoons grated Parmesan cheese
¼ teaspoon cayenne pepper
2 tablespoons olive oil
1 tablespoon clarified butter
Lemon slices, capers, and fresh parsley for garnish

Pound veal slices until very thin. Sprinkle with salt, very lightly. Dredge in flour. Dip in mixture of eggs and water. Press in seasoned bread crumbs. (The Prince Solms uses Pepperidge Farms French rolls cut into small pieces, dried in moderate oven, and crumbled into fine crumbs in food processor.) Add the Parmesan and cayenne pepper to one food processor–load of dried bread.

Heat saucepan first, then add oil and butter. When hot, but not smoking, place veal in pan. Sauté for 1 minute on each side. Remove and drain on paper towel. Arrange slices of lemon with several capers and sprig of parsley on each schnitzel.

The
Redlands
Palestine

When the Redlands opened in 1915, the hotel was hailed as "modern in every detail." You can just imagine how impressive it was to have a telephone, lavatory, and hot water in every room. Probably even more impressive was the fact that many rooms had their own private baths. Four years later, this modern hotel closed its doors, never to be open for guests again.

For years, the Redlands was used as general offices for the International and Great Northern Railroad. When the train era ended, so did the Redlands, and the building stood empty, a forgotten derelict in downtown Palestine.

Twenty years of neglect took its toll on the interior. When Jean Laughlin and her brother Robert bought the old hulk in 1976, they hoped to restore it and make the huge white elephant once again the pride of Palestine. But, as in all restoration projects, even though the purchase price might have been right, the initial cost of the building was merely a snowflake on the tip of the iceberg.

Jean opened an antique shop, several businesses rented space in the structure, and Robert ran the Landmark Restaurant. None of the ventures proved profitable enough to finance large-scale restoration. Jean has moved on to marketing her original gift items made from antique spinning spools and shoe lasts. Robert runs a small private club in the hotel, and the Landmark is now Chang's Chinese Restaurant. Even though Jean and her husband, Norman Mollard, are the only people using the hotel rooms, they hope someday to restore at least one or two floors for guests. At least the Redlands is not doomed to another twenty years of desertion.

Phoenix Chicken

Serves 4

When Jean Laughlin sent in this recipe she wrote, "It is most difficult to choose one dish over another in Chang's — it is all so good. After considerable tasting, Norman and I singled out the Phoenix Chicken. When I asked Chang for his recipe, he replied, 'O.K.,' but when I didn't get it, I realized he didn't understand the word *recipe*. So, I took pen and pad into their kitchen and made my own as he prepared the dish. Mr. Chang is from Taiwan and has not mastered English. Here is his recipe as I watched it prepared before enjoying it."

2 large chicken breasts
1 egg, lightly beaten
1 cup flour, lightly salted
1 cup ham, finely chopped

Take breasts and split. Fill with finely chopped ham. Dip in egg and salted flour. Deep fry in very hot oil for about 3 to 5 minutes or until done. Cut each breast into three pieces crosswise.

Prepare these vegetables to your taste and mix on a large platter. (The vegetables are fresh and raw. The chestnuts and bamboo shoots are canned.)

Broccoli
Chestnuts
Mushrooms
Bamboo shoots
Carrots
Place chicken on top.

Sauce
1 tablespoon vegetable oil
1 garlic clove, chopped
1 tablespoon white wine
1 cup chicken broth
½ teaspoon salt
1 tablespoon sugar
2 tablespoons oyster sauce
2 tablespoons corn starch
1 tablespoon sesame oil
2 tablespoons green onions, chopped

160

Make the sauce in a very hot wok. Mix the ingredients quickly, one at a time in the above order, except for green onions. All must be ready and laid out in a row. Stir until a medium thickness, then add green onions.

Stir 20 seconds and pour over chicken breasts. Serve hot.

Lemon Bread

Yields 1 loaf

½ cup soft margarine
1 cup sugar
1 large lemon
2 eggs, beaten
½ cup milk
1½ cups flour
1 teaspoon baking powder
½ teaspoon salt
½ cup nuts, black walnuts or pecans
¼ cup confectioners' sugar

Cream margarine and sugar until fluffy. Grate peel of lemon and add to mixture. Squeeze juice of lemon and set aside. Add eggs and milk; stir well. Add flour, baking powder, and salt. Stir in nuts. Pour into greased and floured loaf pan. Bake at 350° for 30 to 40 minutes. Pour confectioners' sugar over hot loaf and let it absorb. After 20 minutes, turn onto rack to cool.

Spinach-Mushroom Salad

Serves 4

1 pound fresh spinach
½ pound fresh mushrooms
1 hard-cooked egg yolk
1 small clove garlic, crushed
¼ cup red wine vinegar
¾ cup cooking oil
1 teaspoon salt
1 teaspoon sugar
1 teaspoon black pepper
1 medium onion, chopped

Remove spinach stems, wash, and pat dry. Then tear into bite-sized pieces. Quickly rinse mushrooms in cold water and drain well. Slice thin. Combine egg yolk, garlic, vinegar, oil, sugar, salt, and pepper and blend well. Combine spinach, mushrooms, and onions and toss with egg-yolk mixture.

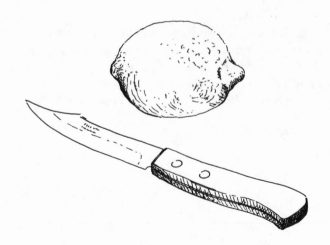

Roper
House
Marble Falls

When Don and Michelle Gunn restored the Roper House, they never dreamed they would be in the restaurant business themselves. The Roper House was leased to someone else, and the Gunns just wanted to save one of Marble Falls' historic buildings. A year later Don and Michelle found out the joys and sorrows of becoming restaurant owners and managers when they took over the business.

Located on busy U.S. Highway 281, which used to see a lot of cattle winding up the Chisholm Trail, the Roper House was built in 1899 by George and Elizabeth Hockenhull Roper. Marble Falls was busy quarrying granite for the State Capitol, and it was also a stage stop, so the Roper House was busy. Along with the drummers, Governor Hogg was a guest of the Ropers.

The Roper House is a marvelous piece of early Texana, and the exterior has been restored to exactly the way George and Elizabeth built it. The interior was gutted completely and converted into large dining rooms upstairs and down. On the second floor is a large bar and club.

Decorated in shades of maroon and pink with brass chandeliers, ceiling fans, and old-fashioned wallpaper, the Roper House offers the same hospitality and good food that made it famous at the turn of the century.

Pecan Pie

Yields 1 9-inch pie

A real Texas dessert is pecan pie. After all, Texas is one of the leading pecan-producing states in the country, and the state tree is the pecan. If those are not enough reasons to eat pecans, Michelle Gunn's tasty and easy recipe is.

3 eggs
⅔ cup sugar
½ teaspoon salt
⅓ cup margarine, melted
1 cup light corn syrup
1 cup pecan pieces or halves

Mix all ingredients. Pour into unbaked 9-inch pie shell and bake 40 to 50 minutes at 375°.

Hotel
Santa Fe
Cleburne

Fortunately, the state of Texas is filled with people who yearn to restore old hotels and create a special bit of nostalgia for others to share and enjoy. One of the aspirants for a trip back into yesteryear is Robert Newton, who purchased the decrepit Hotel Santa Fe in Cleburne.

The name indicates quite clearly the original role of the hotel — to accommodate travelers on the Atchison, Topeka & Santa Fe Railroad. For 3,923 miles the Santa Fe's tracks crisscrossed Texas. Originally the line was just the Atchison & Topeka, bu the Santa Fe was added to indicate that it really followed parts of the historic Santa Fe Trail.

"Under development" (which means it will be finished whenever Robert acquires a lot of financial backing) is Newton Place, which includes the Hotel Santa Fe, Round 'n' Round Antiques, Cafe Coqui, and Jack the Barber. Jack's is the only establishment actually open.

Robert describes his purchase in glowing terms: "Just beneath the original pressed tin ceiling, one can sense the tingle of an earlier Texas railroad town. . . . From the second floor, one can look out on the Santa Fe line still in operation since 1881."

You truly have to admire Robert Newton for his monumental undertaking and wish him the greatest success in the world. His enthusiasm is infectious when he writes: "The hotel has a walk-up lobby which has a unique spired skylight, hammered glass top and sides. The pressed tin ceiling pattern continues up to the skylight. Pine floors . . . all rooms have transoms. The spired skylight has a window which in the summer provided an updraft. Ceiling fans were added later. The 3½ store locations downstairs are having installed 8-foot solid oak doors and panels salvaged from the renovation of the Tarrant County Court House in Fort Worth including the original solid brass hardware."

For the store area, Robert has big dreams. Cleburne is a grand town in Texas and could use a terrific tourist attraction like Newton Place. We hope the town and the thousands of Texans who love old buildings will give Robert the encouragement and support he so rightly deserves. When Cafe Coqui opens, it is obvious you will be served absolutely marvelous food, for the following recipes were outstanding.

Asparagus Pudding

Serves 6 to 8

When you see the delicate white blooms of the lily of the valley, it is difficult to imagine that its close relative is the sturdy asparagus. Lilies of the valley are lovely to behold, but for a superb side dish for any entrée, asparagus is an elegant choice. While most chefs prefer it steamed with a light hollandaise sauce, the Cafe Coqui of the Hotel Santa Fe has devised a unique dish for the canned version of this accompaniment to any main course.

½ cup evaporated milk
½ cup water from canned asparagus
2 slices white bread, crust removed
1 14½-ounce can green asparagus
6 eggs
2 teaspoons butter or margarine, melted
1 cup fresh Parmesan cheese, grated
½ cup mayonnaise
2 hard-boiled eggs, yolks only

Preheat oven to 325°. Grease and flour a 9-inch round mold. Combine evaporated milk and asparagus water. Soak bread slices in this mixture. Blend milk mixture, bread, asparagus, eggs, butter, and Parmesan cheese at high speed in blender for 1 minute. Pour mixture in greased and floured mold. Bake 35 to 40 minutes. Cool in pan and refrigerate until serving. At serving, top with layer of mayonnaise and mashed egg yolks.

Pumpkin Soup

Serves 6 to 8

One of our favorite autumn dishes is pumpkin pie. What would a traditional Thanksgiving dinner be without this American dessert? Then there is pumpkin bread, which is delicious, but for a super harvesttime dish, try a steaming bowl of pumpkin soup.

2½ to 3 cups pumpkin, peeled, seeded, and chopped
7 cups chicken broth
2 large onions, peeled and cut in quarters
3 cloves garlic, diced very fine
¼ cup fresh cilantro, chopped
Sour cream

In large pot, bring all ingredients to a boil. Reduce heat, cover, and simmer for 30 minutes or until pumpkin is soft. Cool a bit and puree in food processor or blender. Return to pot and keep hot. Serve with dab of sour cream.

Note: This recipe was also tried with canned pumpkin and found delicious.

Pineapple-Zucchini Bread

Yields 2 loaves

4 eggs
1½ cups sugar
¾ cup vegetable oil
1½ cups crushed pineapple in syrup
2 cups zucchini, shredded
3¼ cups all-purpose flour
1 teaspoon salt
1½ teaspoons baking powder
1½ teaspoons soda
½ teaspoon ground cloves
2½ teaspoons cinnamon
¾ cup pecans, chopped (optional)

Heat oven to 350°. Grease and flour bottom of two 9 x 5-inch bread pans. In large bowl, beat eggs at high speed until thick. Add sugar gradually. Stir in oil, pineapple, and zucchini. Stir in remaining ingredients. Mix well. Pour batter into pans. Bake at 350° for 45 to 55 minutes. Check for doneness by inserting knife in center. Bread will be ready if knife comes out clean. Cool 15 minutes. Remove from pans.

Glaze
In small bowl, blend 1 cup confectioners' sugar with 2 to 3 tablespoons pineapple juice; spread over warm loaves.

St. Anthony Hotel
San Antonio

The magnificent St. Anthony has recently undergone a massive face-lift, and the grand old lady has emerged more beautiful than ever. Even though the hotel was built in 1909, the St. Anthony really took her rightful place among America's great hotels when she was purchased in 1936 by millionaire rancher R. W. Morrison.

Morrison traveled the world buying priceless antiques and treasures for his hotel. Lavish chandeliers dripping with crystal prisms gleam softly over masterpieces of art, handwoven rugs, and a pure rosewood piano, which Morrison acquired for $27,000, a rather hefty sum in Depression days. The piano's keys originally played for guests at the Russian Embassy in Paris, and now they are played by members of the Morin family for the St. Anthony's visitors.

The St. Anthony (the Anglo translation of San Antonio) became so regal and opulent that San Antonio's most beautiful women came here to see and be seen in the lobby's glittering array of wealth. This parade of finery and beauty gave the lobby the nickname "Peacock Alley," which remains today. It became a San Antonio tradition to meet "under the eagle," the huge oil painting by Claud McCann of an eagle poised for the hunt, which still hangs on the far wall of Peacock Alley.

National travel writers agreed that the St. Anthony, with its museum-quality art and fine service, was one of the most distinctive hotels in the United States. As the years passed, the hotel's reputation was preserved, and the St. Anthony became one of three hotels fifty years old or older still to win national acclaim. Only the Waldorf-Astoria in New York and the Fairmont in San Francisco are in the league of the St. Anthony.

St. Anthony Club Seafood Chowder

Serves 6 to 8

4 ounces bacon
3 ounces leeks
3 ounces potatoes
6 ounces grouper (or other fish)
3 ounces diced clams
12 mussels
Worcestershire sauce, salt, and pepper
3 quarts fish stock or fish bouillon
1 pint heavy cream

Dice raw bacon and sauté until half-cooked. Add diced leeks and small cubed potatoes. Stir constantly, adding fish products, Worcestershire sauce, salt, and pepper. Finish by adding fish stock or fish bouillon to taste. Cook until potatoes are tender. Season to taste. Add heavy cream last, then serve.

St. Anthony Club Chocolate Mousse

Serves 12

8 ounces bitter chocolate
4 ounces sweet chocolate
14 egg yolks
11 ounces granulated sugar
1 quart whipping cream
10 egg whites
¼ ounce cream of tartar
1 ounce coffee liqueur
1 ounce brandy

Melt bitter chocolate with sweet chocolate. Set aside to cool slightly. Whip egg yolks with 5 ounces sugar; put in a bowl. Whip egg whites with 6 ounces sugar and cream of tartar. Mix the yolks with the melted chocolate, coffee liqueur, brandy, and whipped cream; fold in egg whites. Chill.

Sutler's Limpia Hotel
Fort Davis

Back in the days when the only inhabitants who loved West Texas were the Comanches and the Apaches, a fort was the main source of survival for pioneers in this hostile land. Forts were useful only for a relatively short time, but for a few decades these stockades played an important role in the saga of the westward movement. An impressive string of forts was established in Texas, and when they outlived their purpose, most fell into ruins. But some settlements that grew up around the fort survived and retained the name, such as Fort Worth, Fort Stockton, and Fort Davis.

Established in 1854, Fort Davis was named for the secretary of war at the time: Jefferson Davis. Here was the site of the great camel experiment. Those ornery old dromedaries adapted well to the American version of the Sahara Desert, but the Civil War arrived before a western edition of the *Arabian Nights* could be written. During the Civil War the Comanches practically destroyed the outpost, but when the war was over, Union forces arrived with black troopers known as Buffalo Soldiers. The troops distinguished themselves in the line of duty, and Fort Davis was a major defense against the Indians.

Once the Indian question was settled, it seemed as though the town would become as useless as the fort was, because of its remote area. However, tourists found out in those early days what marvelous climate and scenery this oasis had to offer, and the little town became a somewhat famous health resort. A hotel became a necessity, and a group of local merchants constructed the Lympia. (Even though the nearby creek was the Limpia, the hotel was then the Lympia.)

In 1912 the Lympia wa a first-class hotel, but as time passed it housed offices and apartments. Finally, in 1972, the building was restored by the late J. C. Duncan as a hotel once again, this time as the Limpia.

Duncan was a dedicated teacher and inspired his class to research historic Fort Davis to discover how it looked in the past. From the interest generated by a high school assignment, Fort Davis citizens began to restore other buildings. The state of Texas also recognized the value of the fort itself and made it a showcase museum. With all of this restoration, the tourists returned to Fort Davis, for the air is still invigorating and the scenery is still spectacular. Of course, the Limpia is the best place in town.

Rooms at this wonderful little hotel are charming, furnished in oak and tastefully decorated in shades of blue to blend with the Axminster carpet. Downstairs is a homey lobby and one of the best sun porches in Texas. Here you can rock and relax and watch the unhurried world of Fort Davis pass by. The Limpia has proved so popular that an annex has been opened in an adjoining restored building.

Part of the Limpia is the Sutler's Store. If you have watched a few western movies you know that a sutler was the civilian who kept on hand items that were not part of a soldier's regular ration. No doubt the sutler ended up with most of a private's $21-a-month salary. This Sutler's Store is a modern gift shop with delightful items "on hand" for tourists.

The hotel restaurant is the Boarding House, which serves good country dishes, and all that fresh mountain air gives Fort Davis visitors a hearty appetite indeed. There is also a private club at the Boarding House, and hotel guests are given free memberships.

This grand little complex is now owned by Max and Judy Sproul. Max is "on hand" most of the time, for Judy is a schoolteacher, but both have continued a Texas tradition that is hard to beat.

Buttermilk Pie

Yields 1 9-inch pie

3 whole eggs
2 cups sugar
¼ cup melted butter
1 cup buttermilk
3 heaping tablespoons flour
1 teaspoon vanilla
1 unbaked 9-inch pie shell

Cream sugar and butter. Add flour and eggs. Add buttermilk and vanilla. Bake in pie shell at 350° until set (40 to 50 minutes).

Flaky Pie Crust

Makes 5 single crusts

4 cups flour
1 ¾ cups shortening
1 tablespoon sugar
2 teaspoons salt
½ cup water
1 tablespoon vinegar
1 egg

Mix first 4 ingredients with fork. In small bowl, beat ½ cup water and remaining ingredients. Add to first mixture and blend with a fork until dry ingredients are moistened. Mold dough into 5 balls and chill 15 minutes before rolling out. Freezes well.

French Silk Pie

Yields 1 9-inch pie

½ cup butter
¾ cup sugar
1 square unsweetened chocolate, melted
2 eggs
1 teaspoon vanilla
1 baked 9-inch pie shell

Beat butter and sugar until sugar is dissolved. Add melted chocolate, eggs, and vanilla. Beat until light and fluffy. Pour into pie shell. Refrigerate until well chilled. Top with whipped topping and chocolate curls (or grated chocolate).

Tarpon Inn
Port Aransas

Though not the place for the weary businessman in search of the comforts of the Hyatt Regency or Ramada Inn, the Tarpon Inn is a getaway from a "world [that] is too much with us." Its accommodations are of the past, very beachy, and racked by the salt air and years of use, but from its decks you can discover the true meaning of the saying that at the sea, time is endless. Sit on the balcony and watch the tankers and shrimpers, or simply contemplate the really big one you're going to catch the next day. The die-hard fisherman could not ask for more.

The Tarpon Inn, now on the National Register of Historic Places, was built in 1886 by Frank Stephenson, a boat pilot and assistant Aransas Lighthouse keeper. He constructed it in an old Civil War barracks. In 1897 Stephenson sold it to Mary Cotter and her son J. E., who built two new structures after the original burned in 1900. When the 1919 hurricane destroyed the main building, J. M. Ellis, the third owner, rebuilt her to resemble the old barracks. Ellis put twenty-foot poles in sixteen feet of concrete, with pilings at the corner of each room for reinforcement. As a result of this strong construction, the inn has provided shelter for area residents during storms and has served as headquarters for the Red Cross, Salvation Army, and military units. Since the 1920s, nothing much has changed at the Tarpon Inn except for some 1950 refurbishing; recently some of the downstairs rooms have been updated. There are still no televisions or phones in the small rooms, and the entire place is in need of a coat of paint. You'll love owner-lawyer Jim Atwill, though. He has a gracious personality that compensates for a few inconveniences here and there.

Once a retreat for people from the King Ranch, the Tarpon Inn has also hosted such notables as Billy Mitchell and Aimee Semple McPherson, who reportedly spent most of her time on the phone managing her investments. Some of the most memorable guests have included a group of college professors who used their Phi Beta Kappa keys as tarpon lures and a multimillionaire who brought his own tankful of goldfish as bait. But the most famous was Franklin D. Roosevelt, who came to fish for tarpon in 1937. The Presidential Suite is a composite of rooms where FDR stayed. Proof of his visit can be found on the wall of the lobby, where the former president signed and dated his tarpon scale, which is incidentally the largest of 7,500 tarpon scales that are mounted on the wall. A great 1937 photo of FDR accompanies the scale, with the caption, "President Roosevelt tells a fish story." Among the famous signatures are the names of anglers representing every state in the nation and twenty-one foreign countries.

As for the food, Duncan Hines spent his honeymoon here and recommended the food for twenty-five years. The seafood is fresh and very tastefully prepared as only coastal residents know how. The stuffed shrimp and the bowl of "U-peel-um" are especially delicious. The restaurant decor is a real Gulf education, with giant stuffed tarpon over the bar as well as such giant trophies as redfish, kingfish, and wahoo.

If it's fishing for tarpon in the summer, duck hunting in the fall and winter, or simply beachcombing that brings you to Port Aransas, the shrimp capital of Texas, consider the Tarpon Inn. The picturesque art colony of Rockport is only ten miles away, and Aransas National Wildlife Refuge, winter home of the endangered whooping crane, is thirty-five miles to the north. You can be sure that your stay at the Tarpon Inn will be a memorable one.

Authentic Gazpacho

Serves 8 to 10

Below, Jim Atwill adds his personal touches to the following recipe.

Shopping List
1 head celery
3 No. 300 cans (14½ ounces each) peeled plum tomatoes
Tops of green onions or chives or scallions (7 to 12 tops)
1 large green pepper
2 small cucumbers
White bread (preferably firm-type bread like Pepperidge Farm)
2 fresh tomatoes, optional and if available

Staples
Salt
Black pepper
3 or 4 cloves garlic
Olive oil
Some kind of sherry (either cocktail or cooking)
White vinegar

I find that the best container to prepare and mix in, store in, and serve from is a one-gallon cookie jar, which you can pick up at most stores in the glassware section.

First slice up the cloves of garlic and mash with a wooden pestle on the bottom of the jar. Then add 2 or 3 slices of bread and to that ⅓ cup vinegar and ⅓ cup sherry until the bread is thoroughly soaked and will absorb no more. Then with wooden pestle mash the bread into the garlic, adding 5 tablespoons of olive oil, just enough to make a smooth paste. Blend in one of the tomatoes after cutting tomatoes up either by knife or with scissors and mashing thoroughly.

Add the vegetables (6 to 7 stalks of celery, with a few of its leaves more finely chopped, the green pepper, the 7 to 12 tops of onions or scallions, cucumber sliced with the rind, and tomatoes if desired). Extreme accuracy of measurement is not required, and the vegetables should all be coarsely chopped, since they will be eaten with a spoon. The Cuisinart food processor with the top slicing blade is ideal for this type of chopping. Add salt and black pepper to taste, remembering that they will be partly absorbed by the vegetables. Stir well and add the remaining cans of peeled plum tomatoes, again after cutting up the tomatoes in the can with either scissors or a knife.

As the gazpacho is normally prepared a day in advance and refrigerated for at least 24 hours, the next operation requires judgment, which comes from the experience of making the dish a few times. At the time of mixing the gazpacho, it may taste bland, but by the next day it will have developed a sharp and exciting flavor. First the jar must be filled up with the right balance of flavoring liquid. Add enough water to the already prepared mixture; fill it up approximately 1½ inches from the top of the jar. Stir, taste, and add salt if necessary, and then cover and let sit for 24 hours. The next day if it is still too bland, add another can of peeled plum tomatoes and salt and pepper and stir. If too strong, then add more water. Cover and refrigerate, and your gazpacho should last as long as three weeks without loss of flavor or crispness of the diced vegetables.

Thomas Jefferson Rusk Hotel
Rusk

The Thomas Jefferson Rusk Hotel has been standing solidly on the courthouse square in Rusk since the mid-1920s. In fact, the building is so strong that when it was once considered expendable, the former owners decided it would cost too much to tear down the 18-inch walls. The old structure was closed from 1978 until March 18, 1983, when it reopened after a $500,000 face-lift by Richard and Diane Lowden.

The Lowdens retained Luis Pereira, a Los Angeles hotel architect and designer, who was concerned with preserving the nostalgic twenties mood of the hotel. The red and white brick exterior of the building was cleaned and repaired, and green awnings were added. Bricks were added to the sidewalks around the hotel to add more personality to the setting.

The interior color scheme revolves around different shades of brown, with the walnut, cinnamon, and beige hues so popular of the decade that preceded the Great Depression. The lobby, with its maroon Oriental rug, Art Nouveau chandelier, terrazzo floors, and Queen Anne chairs, provides a very comfortable atmosphere in which guests may congregate.

Mr. Pereira also added mood throughout the hotel by using wallpaper of subtle little prints and stripes, wood moldings, and tile floors to accent the high ceilings. All thirty-six rooms are furnished with lovely brass beds, light-filtering curtains, and custom-designed carpets.

The only remaining original piece of furniture is the massive oak veneer desk used for registering guests. F. Scott Fitzgerald's Jay Gatsby would have been right at home in the hotel's dining room, affectionately called T. J.'s, with its romantic pink walls and tablecloths, subtle lighting, and brass fixtures, or in the Sam Houston Club, with its color scheme of salmon and jade.

Historians will love the city of Rusk, for it has thirteen sites eligible for historical markers. It is assumed that a blacksmith's shop once stood where the hotel is now; when excavation took place, five horseshoes and a pistol were found that date back to the 1800s. Luckily there is accurate documentation of other Rusk sites where history was made. For example, the J. W. Summers House was built in 1884 by convict labor with bricks made by hand from clay in the cellar. The Perkins Home, built in 1861, sports a historical marker. This two-story white house is next to the Footbridge, also a marked site, which has been called the longest footbridge in the nation. The wood carvings on the front gable of the home depict a star and a rising sun, which are symbols of the Lone Star state.

The most interesting attraction in Rusk, of course, is the Texas State Railroad, a Texas Parks and Wildlife Department project dedicated to the preservation of the steam locomotive and the railroad's golden age. Tourists can actually take the 25.5-mile ride on the antique train from Rusk to Palestine. Be sure to notice the giant painting of a train on the red brick building on Fifth Street, one block southeast of the hotel. After using many gallons of acrylic medium and varnish, local artist Lynn Brown completed the scene in eleven months, but only after working seven to eight hours a day through wind, rain, and cold. She did much of the work high on a scaffolding. She often tied around her waist a rope that was secured by hooks to keep her from blowing off. After seeing Lynn's painting, also see the Frazer Home, the Gregg Home, and the fifty-year-old Methodist and Presbyterian churches.

The following recipes were contributed by the James Perkins family, very prominent long-time residents of Rusk.

Pea and Peanut Salad

Serves 4

1 package frozen small English peas
½ cup mayonnaise
¼ teaspoon Worchestershire sauce
2 tablespoons celery, finely chopped
Dash garlic powder and salt
1 tablespoon green onion, finely chopped
Juice of ½ lemon
1 small can Planters Spanish Peanuts

Defrost peas until half-thawed. Combine all ingredients with peas except peanuts. Just before serving, add peanuts, skins and all. The peanuts add the needed salt and a delightful crunch.

Marylyn Perkins Buie, Jim Perkins's sister, submitted this different recipe. She found that this was not a favorite of children, many of whom are not pea eaters, but adults love it!

Hermits from California

Yields 40 to 60 cookies

3 egg whites
1 cup sugar
1 pound pitted dates, chopped
1 cup pecan pieces
1 cup flour
1 teaspoon baking powder
Pinch of salt
1½ teaspoons vanilla
1 teaspoon fresh lemon juice

Beat egg whites, not too stiff. Add vanilla and lemon juice. Add sugar, dates, nuts, flour, salt, and baking powder last. It is important to mix in this order. Drop from teaspoon onto greased and floured cookie sheet. Bake in moderate oven (350°) 15 minutes. When cool, put in tin box.

Recipe of Myrta Perkins Kerr, born in 1892, aunt of James I. Perkins.

Aunt May's Chocolate Cake

Yields 3 9-inch layers

This hundred-year-old recipe originated with May Buchanan, Aunt May to Howard Hoover, father-in-law of James I. Perkins. Frank Buchanan was president of the bank in Hardin and was a wheat and soybean farmer.

6 tablespoons cocoa
1 cup boiling water
2 cups sugar
½ cup butter
2 eggs, separated
2½ cups cake flour
2 teaspoons soda
Pinch salt
1 cup buttermilk
1 teaspoon vanilla

Cook cocoa and water together until thick. Cool. Cream together sugar and butter. Add egg yolks to butter and sugar and cream again. Sift together flour, soda, and salt. Mix dry ingredients alternately with buttermilk, beginning and ending with dry ingredients. Add the cooled cocoa mixture and vanilla to the batter and fold in stiffly beaten egg whites. Grease and flour three 9-inch cake pans. Cut waxed paper to fit the pans and line the already prepared pans if desired to prevent sticking. Bake at 350° for 25 to 30 minutes.

Icing
Melt in a double boiler:
3 ounces chocolate
2 tablespoons butter

Combine in a blender or mixer with:
2¾ cups sifted confectioners' sugar
½ teaspoon salt
1 teaspoon vanilla
6 tablespoons light cream

Combine with the butter and chocolate mixture in double boiler and heat for 10 minutes. Add 1 teaspoon vanilla. If stiff, blend in 1 tablespoon cream.

Traveler's Hotel
Denison

There are all sorts of reasons to visit the Traveler's Hotel. It is an absolutely marvelous old building that Bob and Betty Brandt have restored into an inn and restaurant. You can appreciate the architecture and decor, stay in one of their three charming guest rooms furnished in antiques, or sample their gourmet food. (Bob is a graduate of Le Cordon Bleu.) Take those three ingredients, blend them together, and you have the perfect recipe for a country inn.

Denison has always been a railroad town, and back in the golden age of trains, six different lines pulled into the station every day. To withstand all that rumble and roar, buildings near the tracks had to be extremely solid and sturdy. So when a German immigrant named Ernest Martin Kohl built his home in 1893 down by the station, he had the walls constructed two feet thick. The trains have long ceased shaking the Kohl home, but it stands just as firm as the day it was completed.

Kohl, a former sea captain, made his fortune in the grocery business, and his home was very elegant, with handsome paneled walls. His wine cellar was well stocked, and he devised ingenious fire-prevention methods for the roof. After all, trains threw a lot of hot cinders at the turn of the century.

After a few years, Kohl turned his huge four-story mansion into the "Traveler's Home," and guests practically got off the train at the front door. The Brandts' guests are just a few steps from the tracks as well, but don't worry about the noise. The tracks are just as empty as the station across the street. Plans are under way to develop this wonderful old station into shops sometime in the uncertain future.

The restaurant decor is an eclectic assortment of antiques and gigantic stuffed wild-game trophies. You can dine in Papa Kohl's old wine cellar and read the Kohl family names signed on the bricks, or perhaps in the section that once housed the buggy. It doesn't matter where you sit in this charming restaurant; the food is always fantastic, for Bob is the chef. There is no doubt he graduated from Le Cordon Bleu at the head of his class with honors. *Bon appétit!*

Chicken Breast Suprême

Serves 4

Prepare four chicken breasts by removing all bones and skin. Season with salt and white pepper. Top each breast with lots of butter. Bake in 350° oven for 12 minutes or until done. Top the breasts with suprême sauce and garnish with wild rice.

Suprême Sauce
2 tablespoons butter
2 tablespoons flour
1 cup whole milk
3 tablespoons dry sherry

Melt butter in saucepan and stir in flour to make roux. Add milk and simmer for 10 minutes, being careful not to scorch. Add sherry and keep warm until ready to serve.

Veal Cordon Bleu

Serves 4

4 veal cutlets
4 thin slices ham
4 thin slices Swiss cheese
Salt, white pepper
Thyme
Flour
Butter
Peanut oil

Prepare cutlets by pounding flat. Remove all fat and tissue. Fold cutlets in half and stuff each with one slice of ham and one slice of cheese. Season with salt, pepper, and thyme. Dredge the stuffed cutlets in flour and sauté in butter and peanut oil over high flame until brown on both sides. Remove and serve at once with pasta or wild rice.

Stuffed Gourmet Tomatoes

Serves 4

4 large tomatoes
Salt
Pepper
8 ounces cream cheese
Parmesan cheese
Bread crumbs
Butter

Select four large ripe tomatoes and cut off tops and bottoms so they will sit flat on the dish and not roll. Hollow out cores and season shells with salt and pepper. Then stuff with cream cheese and sprinkle the tops with Parmesan cheese and bread crumbs. Dribble one teaspoon of butter on the top of each tomato before baking at 350° for 12 minutes or until hot. Serve promptly.

Victorian
Inn
Galveston

If you have ever wondered what it was like living at the turn of the century, you simply have to visit the Victorian Inn on 17th Street in Galveston. On the National Register of Historic Places, she still stands, massive and graceful, with her 1899 stained-glass windows still intact despite coastal winds and summer hurricanes. In fact, this house is even a survivor of the Great Hurricane of 1900, a testimony to the fine, detailed workmanship that seems so absent today.

The phrase "You can't go home again" certainly doesn't hold true for the old Isaac Hefron home. The red and white structure with its wraparound porch, three balconies, and inviting swing seems to beckon you. When you walk through those massive front doors, you *are* home. The antique furnishings, intricately carved stairwell rails, the wooden lacework trim, and the warmth of the young managers, Loreen and Darrell John, all beg you to stay and stay.

Owner Don Mafridge must have felt this warmth, too, because he has put much money and time into this showplace, which was originally built by concrete contractor Isaac Hefron in 1899. The restoration is so complete that the Victorian Inn has been featured on the Galveston Historical Foundation's Tour of Homes. There are three floors, the first two open to guests. The guest floors comprise four suites, with one bath for each two suites.

A large, cheery foyer opens on one side to a spacious dining room with large beachy windows, an added period chandelier, and original hardwood pegged floors. It is here that caterer-manager Loreen serves hot coffee or tea, juice, homemade banana-nut bread, sour cream coffee cake, and other breakfast goodies. If you are really lucky, you will be there during grapefruit season, when the backyard tree yields its crop. If you don't wake up for breakfast, never fear. There's a little off-the-dining-room nook where coffee and sweets are always available with help-yourself service. The continental breakfast is the only meal served.

After breakfast, wander to the other side of the house to the large living room and office to lounge on the comfortable period sofas, visit with the other guests, or simply watch television. Note the lovely Belgian tiled fireplace, one of many in the inn. You may want to play cards or soul-search while sitting in the curious little nook near the stairway with its finely carved and scrolled arm rests. This area was probably built for the Hefron children, whose names are used to designate the bedrooms upstairs. Hefron also named a room for himself: Isaac's Room. This guest bedroom, beautifully decorated with nineteenth-century decor, is the only one of the four with twin beds. The others are equipped with king-sized beds, and all are air-conditioned and heated. Two rooms have private balconies (there is a screened one in Isaac's Room), and two others share the third balcony. Amy's Room has a small addition with a single bed. Plenty of light shines in every room because of huge, breezy windows, some of which are walk-throughs to the balconies.

Former Houstonians Loreen and Darrell are the newest members of the Victorian Inn staff, having been managers since the summer of 1983. Darrell, a professional singer, helps with routine chores and the many responsibilities that go with managing an inn. Loreen caters parties and weddings, so both are skilled in the art of hospitality and entertainment.

As for the delights that follow, they are Loreen's special favorites, which she often serves her guests. To taste the real thing, however, call the Johns for a reservation at the Victorian Inn. It will be one of the most relaxing visits you will ever experience.

Sour Cream Coffee Cake

Yields 1 cake

1 cup margarine
2 cups sugar
2 eggs
½ cup sour cream
2½ teaspoons vanilla
2 cups cake flour, sifted
1¼ teaspoons baking powder
¼ teaspoon salt
Confectioners' sugar

Combine margarine, sugar, and eggs. Add sour cream and vanilla. Beat well. Fold in sifted dry ingredients. Pour half the batter in well-greased and floured angel-food cake pan. Spread half the topping over this. Add rest of batter and topping. Bake at 350° for 1 hour. While warm sprinkle with confectioners' sugar. Cool completely in pan.

Topping
2 tablespoons sugar
½ cup nuts
½ teaspoon cinnamon

Fresh Apple Bread

Yields 1 loaf

1 cup sugar
½ cup margarine
2 eggs, beaten
1 cup grated apple
2 cups all-purpose flour
1 teaspoon baking soda
½ teaspoon vanilla
1½ tablespoons milk (or buttermilk)
1 cup nuts, chopped
3 tablespoons sugar
1 teaspoon cinnamon

Cream sugar and margarine. Add eggs and apple. Mix in the dry ingredients. Add vanilla and milk and nuts. Pour into lightly greased loaf pan. Sprinkle with mixture of sugar and cinnamon. Bake at 350° 1 hour for large loaf pan, or 30 to 35 minutes for 2 small pans.

Cranberry Nut Bread

Yields 1 loaf

2 cups flour, sifted
½ cup sugar
3 teaspoons baking powder
1 teaspoon salt
¼ teaspoon soda
1 teaspoon cinnamon
½ cup chopped walnuts
1 egg, beaten
1 cup canned whole cranberry sauce, drained
1 teaspoon orange peel, grated
2 tablespoons shortening, melted

Sift together dry ingredients. Combine egg, cranberry sauce, orange peel, and shortening. Blend in dry ingredients and nuts; stir until just moistened. Mixture will be thick. Pour into greased 9 x 5 x 3-inch loaf pan. Bake in moderate oven (350°) for 45 to 50 minutes. Cool on rack.

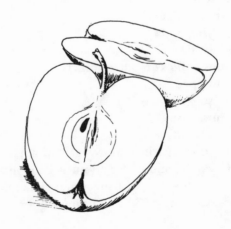

Von Minden Hotel
Schulenberg

In 1926 Egon Von Minden decided to open a long-awaited movie theater in the quiet little town of Schulenberg. It was designed to show the latest silent movies and also to accommodate live productions. Egon built dressing rooms, an orchestra pit, and even a glass-paneled "crying room" for the patrons' disgruntled babies. He bought the best sound system (now a museum piece) and projectors (they have been modernized somewhat). Egon's creation is still in use today as the Cozy Theater.

A year later Egon built and opened the Von Minden Hotel. He utilized his property to the fullest, for the Von Minden totally enclosed the Cozy. To keep it in the family, Egon's daugher Leonida and her husband Irwin Speckel managed the hotel and movie theater. It became the Speckel home for fifty-three years, and the family raised two daughters here. As a result, the building received tender loving care. But as the Von Minden aged, so did Leonida and Irwin, and in 1978 the Von Minden closed. Schulenberg became another "last picture show."

Bill and Betty Pettit, however, saw the hotel's charm and decided to buy it from Leonida and Irwin. By 1980 the Von Minden was alive again because of these two energetic Houstonians. Work began on the hotel's restoration, and all forty-one rooms have now been refurbished. Bill and Betty are still using some of the ancient sheets and towels that Leonida so meticulously mended. Though antiques are being added, the hotel decor is plain. However, all of the rooms are air-conditioned, and twenty have baths. Original ceiling fans and iron beds are still in the rooms, and a few even have television sets.

There are no phones, but the desk clerk will see that you get ice, coffee, and a meal served in your room. The Pettits have kept the lobby as it was in the 1920s, with the original front desk, key rack, and several old writing desks. The original old register is also still there, with everyone listed who has ever stayed at the hotel.

Bill, who has a law practice in Houston, races back and forth from Houston to Schulenberg so he can work the theater projector. The Cozy Theater seems to be his biggest interest. And no wonder! It is full of personality, with its old wooden seats and stage. There is also a balcony with benches and its own separate entrance that was used years ago for the black community, who were excluded from the main floor. If you ask Bill, he may unroll the old advertisers' oleo, a canvas curtain (still in wonderful shape) with hand-painted 1930 ads for local businesses. Current movies are still shown six nights a week (except Mondays), with a different feature weekly. One night a month the Pettits show a classic movie starring such greats as Bette Davis or Errol Flynn. Twice a year they host a live concert or performance at the theater. Every spring they also organize a classic film festival, providing a bus ride from Houston to Schulenberg with an overnight package available at reasonable rates.

As for Betty, she not only has her hands full with hotel duties, but she also runs Mama's Pizza Kitchen (Betty is Mama), located in the same building, and the Hard Times Restaurant, which serves steak and seafood. Her pizza kitchen, a very popular spot after the movie, serves pizzas, po-boys, and sandwiches. In addition, Betty serves a continental breakfast to overnight guests, consisting of biscuits, jam, juice, and coffee.

Note that Betty has sent her favorite pizza recipe straight from her kitchen. The pizza is Italian, the town German, and the folks are friendly and hospitable at the Von Minden.

Broccoli Soup

Serves 8

Betty Pettit handles Mama's Pizza Kitchen daily, but on weekends Bill runs the Hard Times Restaurant on the second floor of the hotel. (This used to be the Speckels' apartment.) However, the cooking is done down in the pizza kitchen and hauled up two flights of stairs to guests. Bill, with his white beard, cheery smile, and chunky torso, looks like Santa Claus in jeans serving dinner. But the food is so good that you are glad this version of Santa is around all year.

3 cups chopped broccoli or 3 packages frozen chopped broccoli
1 large onion, quartered
1 large stalk celery, cut in pieces
¼ cup rice
4 cups chicken broth
2 13-ounce cans evaporated milk
1 tablespoon butter or margarine
Salt to taste
Cayenne pepper to taste

In large pot, put broccoli, onion, celery, rice, and chicken broth. Boil until rice is tender. The place ingredients in blender and blend until smooth. Put back into large pot and add milk, butter, and seasonings. Heat and serve.

Note: You can substitute either yellow squash or zucchini for the broccoli, and it is just as good.

Spiced Peaches

Betty says, "This is an old recipe that my mother used to use when we were kids. She was raised in Arkansas where there were fresh peaches in abundance, and when our family moved to the big city (Houston), she made these spiced peaches using canned peaches. They are so good, and you can use the cheapest brand of peaches you can find. It makes them taste just like home-canned; but the secret is to *wait,* at least a week, before you eat them."

1 large can (1 pound, 13 ounces) peach halves
½ cup vinegar
¼ cup brown sugar
1 teaspoon whole cloves
1 cinnamon stick

Boil all ingredients together for about 15 minutes. Then pour into a tightly covered jar and refrigerate, the longer the better.

Mama's Pizza

Makes 4 large pizzas

If you are wondering why a hotel with a German name in a very German town has a pizza specialty, it is because Betty Pettit was in the pizza business before she was in the hotel business. After the Pettits bought the Von Minden, Betty decided that her pizza place should be connected with the hotel. So nestled in the rear of the old Von Minden is Mama's Pizza Kitchen. Betty has shared her particular pizza recipe that goes over big in Schulenberg.

For the dough, Betty says, "Just use your favorite yeast bread recipe or mix. Let rise in a covered bowl. Then, punch down the dough, and press it onto a large greased pizza pan. Dribble over a little olive oil and cover with the sauce."

Sauce
2 1-pound, 12-ounce cans crushed tomatoes
4 15-ounce cans tomato sauce
1 whole clove garlic, peeled
1 whole onion
1 green pepper
1 tablespoon oregano
1 teaspoon sweet basil
Salt to taste

Place all ingredients in blender, a little at a time, and blend until pureed. Simmer about 30 minutes.

Topping
Pour sauce on the crusts and sprinkle generously with grated Romano cheese. Add ¼-inch layer of grated mozzarella or mozzarella slices. Sprinkle oregano lightly on top of mozzarella.

Add your favorite toppings: Italian sausage, hamburger meat, pepperoni, chopped fresh onion, chopped green pepper, sliced ripe olives, sliced mushrooms. Top all ingredients with a light sprinkling of more mozzarella.

Cook in hot oven 450° 30 minutes.

The Warwick
Houston

The majestic Warwick sits on Main Street between Houston's downtown business district and its world-famous medical center. From the top floors, guests can gaze down the city's main artery to the north and see Houston's rapidly growing skyline. They can look to the south and view the gigantic hospital complex, Hermann Park, and Rice University. The view itself is quite famous. The hotel management is proud of the fact that when Phil Donahue asked Bob Hope to choose one place of all his travels that he thought was the prettiest, Hope replied, "In Houston, the view of Main Street from my room in the Warwick Hotel."

The Warwick was constructed in 1926 during the glitter and gaiety of the Roaring Twenties. Its builders, wishing to maintain a stately center for hospitality, decided to use the regal motif; thus the name "the Warwick" after Francis Greville Earle Brooke, the Earl of Warwick Baron Brooke. The original structure consisted of eleven stories containing 360 rooms, 80 of which were reserved for transient guests, while the others comprised 60 apartments ranging from efficiency dwellings to some more than 5,000 square feet. Today, all that remains of the old Warwick is the name and the masonry shell. That is because in 1962 the forty-year-old hotel was sold to the John W. Mecom Company, which renovated it to the tune of $11 million. Mr. Mecom added the north and south sections, including 130 guest rooms and suites, a north and south lobby, a ballroom, two restaurants, meeting rooms, and an elliptical-shaped swimming pool surrounded by lanais — cabana-type guest rooms that look down on the pool from the third floor.

The Warwick Club and the Presidential Suite, both (pardon the cliché) "fit for kings," are on the top and most prestigious floor. The private club, open only to its 2,000 members and hotel guests, provides a breathtaking view of uptown and downtown Houston and of the famous Mecom Fountain. Decorated in royal blue and gold, the Louis XVI furnishings add approximately a crown of lights to this beautiful hotel.

If you can afford it, the Presidential Suite is sensational. It has been occupied by such notable personalities as Queen Beatrix of the Netherlands, Chancellor Helmut Schmidt of West Germany, Frank Sinatra, Andy Warhol, Norman Mailer, and former President Jimmy Carter. Consisting of a drawing-sitting room, a dining area, and four bedrooms with baths, the suite is decorated in silks and damask, marble and Baccarat crystal chandeliers that are irreplaceable. The art, mantlepiece, and antiques housed here date back to the seventeenth and eighteenth centuries. The *pièces de résistance,* however, are four beautifully carved Louis XV panels, representing justice, strength in peace, strength in war, and royalty. They were actually used in the Palace of Versailles until 1830, when Louis Philipe removed them and put them in storage. From 1871 to 1875, they were restored by Casiner Perier. They are obviously works of art, and a guest can enjoy their beauty for a mere $1,000 a night!

But don't despair if you can't afford the price. You may not be able to live like a king, but you can certainly eat like one. Dining at the Warwick is quite a culinary experience; the menu represents cuisine found in every corner of the world. The breakfast menu includes eggs prepared in every way imaginable, including, of course, Eggs Benedict and the Scotsman, an omelet served with smoked salmon, sour cream, and capers. The recommended dish, however, is Bircher Muesli, a heavenly healthful breakfast (*muesli* being a blend of oats, oranges, apricots, grapes, nuts, and sultana raisins). The preparation is named after Dr. Bircher, the famous Swiss nutritionist. It's just the thing for a busy guest in need of a hearty breakfast.

If you sleep through breakfast, never fear; a taste of the world is also offered at lunch. Are you yearning for the hills of Dover? Try Dover Sole "Dora." Perhaps you prefer French or German cuisine. If so, enjoy Baby Chicken "Lafayette" or Wiener schnitzel. The Baked Potato "Mirabelle," however, is especially wonderful. A potato stuffed with shrimp, scallops, and poached egg topped with hollandaise sauce, this recipe was brought to the Warwick by Chef Shiramizu, who served it to British royalty. Dinner in the Hunt Room is truly designed with the hunter at heart. Everything from Wild Boar "Marcassin" to Mallard Duck "Lucullus" and Venison Medallion "St. Hubert" is offered.

The following recipes are some of the best you will find in Texas. They have been given to us by Chef Shiramizu, who is an expert in classic French food, nouvelle cuisine, and the preparation of game. Fluent in several languages, he is a native of Japan who received his professional permit from the government of Japan's Western Cooking School in 1968. Since that time, Chef Shiramizu has held positions in fine hotels and restaurants in Zurich, Munich, London, LeHavre, Toronto, and Ottawa. He was also associated with the three-star Mirabelle Restaurant, Mayfair, London, which has catered to such celebrities as John Wayne, Brigitte Bardot, Charlie Chaplin, Marlon Brando, Paul Newman, and the Baron de Rothschild.

Bircher Muesli

Serves 6

Dr. Bircher was a famed Swiss nutritionist, and he created "the perfect breakfast," which took the Swiss nation by storm. Bircher Muesli (pronounced mew-se-lee) was introduced when the Warwick reopened in 1964, and it is a breakfast favorite with the Warwick's guests. For an absolutely delicious and healthful way to begin any day, try a heaping bowl of *muesli*.

2 cups oatmeal
1½ cups milk
2 apples
Juice of 2 lemons
2 tablespoons granulated sugar
¼ cup raisins
24 grapes
1 cup pineapple, diced
12 fresh strawberries
½ cup almonds
1 cup whipped cream
1 piece banana
½ cup apricots

Combine oatmeal and milk and let rest for 15 minutes. Grate apples and blend immediately with lemon juice and sugar. Add raisins, grapes, pineapple, strawberries, and almonds and mix well. Fold in half the whipped ceram shortly before serving. Garnish with the sliced banana, the apricots, and the rest of the cream.

Baked Potato "Mirabelle"

Serves 4

Chef Takashi Shiramizu created Baked Potato "Mirabelle" during his tenure at the Mirabelle Restaurant, when he was summoned by the executive chef of Buckingham Palace to come and assist in the food preparation during the absence of the palace *sous-chef*. So, if you've always wondered what Queen Elizabeth and Princess Diana enjoy eating, you no longer have to come to the Hunt Room and Cafe Vienna of the Warwick, nor do you have to wait for an invitation to Buckingham Palace. You can just follow this recipe for a dish fit for a queen.

    4 baking potatoes (10 ounces each)
    4 ounces sea scallops
    12 large shrimp, cleaned and deveined
    4 ounces lobster bisque (canned bisque is acceptable)
    4 ounces heavy cream
    4 soft poached eggs (3 minutes)
    1 cup hollandaise sauce

Bake potatoes until done. Cut 1 inch off top and make a cavity by removing the inside of potato, but keep a ⅜-inch wall. Sauté the scallops and shrimp in light butter. Add lobster bisque and cream. Salt and pepper lightly. Bring to a boil. Spoon into potato cavity. Top with a poached egg and cover with hollandaise sauce.

Feta Shrimp "Theo Fanidi"

Serves 4

Heinrich Lutjens, the Warwick's food and beverage manager for nineteen years, received a request from a host who wanted to entertain with a special dinner serving only authentic Greek food. Mr. Lutjens called upon the expertise of his friend, Mr. Theo Fanidi, to assure the dinner's success. The host was delighted with the results, proclaiming the menu creations to be as authentic as any in Greece. Following the dinner, Feta Shrimp "Theo Fanidi" was named in honor of the creator and added to the luncheon entrées available to all diners at the Warwick.

1 pound fresh shrimp, peeled and deveined
2 large tomatoes, peeled and chopped
2 large onions, thinly sliced
1 clove garlic, minced
½ pound feta cheese
2 tablespoons chopped fresh parsley
2 tablespoons olive oil

Sauté onions in olive oil until tender. Add diced tomatoes, garlic, parsley, salt, and pepper. Simmer for 15 minutes. Pour mixture into four ovenproof dishes. Add one-fourth of the shrimp to each dish and sprinkle with olive oil. Top with crumbled feta cheese. Bake at 450° for 15 minutes.

The combination of feta cheese and shrimp is a simple gourmet dish that is absolutely superb.

Farce for a Rattlesnake Pâté

Serves 6

6 ounces rattlesnake meat (other meat may be substituted for the faint-hearted)
6 ounces chicken breast
6 ounces veal, inside round
3 ounces chicken fat
1 ounce brandy
2 eggs
1 cup heavy cream
1 ounce butter
1 teaspoon green peppercorns
Salt and pepper

Cut meats in 1-inch cubes and sauté in chicken fat until medium-rare. Let cool. Pass through meat grinder three times. Place in mixing bowl and gradually work in eggs, cream, and butter. Add brandy, peppercorns, and salt and pepper to taste. Shape into a ball and chill on greased pâté mold; chill until firm.

Baked Lobster Bisque

Serves 6

Chef Shiramizu says that the secrets to the success of this rich cream soup are the whipped cream, sherry, and curry.

2 medium-sized boiled lobsters
2½ cups chicken stock
1 onion, sliced
4 ribs celery leaves
2 whole cloves
1 bay leaf
6 peppercorns
¼ cup butter
¼ cup flour
3 cups milk
½ teaspoon nutmeg
1 cup cream
1 ounce sherry
1 teaspoon curry powder
1 cup whipped cream

Remove meat from lobsters. Dice body meat and mince tail and claw meat. Reserve. Crush shell. Add to them the tough end of the claws and chicken stock, onion, celery leaves, cloves, bay leaf, and peppercorns. Simmer 30 minutes.

When you strain this stock, if there is coral roe, force it through a fine sieve, combine it with butter in a mortar or bowl, add flour and when well blended, pour heated milk slowly on it, stirring until mixture is smooth.

If no roe, melt butter, stir in flour, and gradually add milk and nutmeg. When sauce is smooth and boiling, add lobster and stock. Simmer covered for 5 minutes. Turn off heat, and stir in hot, but not boiling, cream. Pour into baking cups.

To make topping, mix sherry with curry powder and add whipped cream. Broil until lightly browned (2 to 3 seconds).

Weimar
Country
Inn
Weimar

Another country inn, the Weimar Country Inn, has been saved from the jaws of progress by farsighted businessmen Ron Jones of Houston, Carl Halla of Weimar, and twenty limited partnership investors. They saw beauty in the decrepit old hotel, a casualty of changing times and the declining railroad. There is certainly nothing decrepit about it now, for it stands beautifully restored and gracious, a welcome addition to the 1873 railroad town of Weimar.

The Old Jackson Hotel, built in the 1870s to accommodate the needs of weary train travelers who rode on the old Galveston, Harrisburg, and San Antonio line, stood across from the tracks and depot. By 1910 two Jackson Hotels had existed. Vague memory has it that the first either burned or was demolished, but we know for certain that the second was destroyed by a hurricane. In 1910 a new hotel, the San Jacinto Hotel, was erected on the same spot. A twenty-room, one-bath hotel, the San Jacinto had a cypress clapboard facade that was later covered with stucco (around 1939). Before it closed in 1970, it was owned at different times by Henry Brasher, someone named Gray, and Mrs. Dan Connolly, to name a few. After 1970 it was used as a nursing home for a while and was sold to the city, which had planned to tear it down and use the property for a city maintenance yard.

Ron Jones and Carl Halla, however, could not let this happen. With other interested investors, they decided to save the hotel and found architect Clovis Heimsath to renovate her. When the work was finished, the small guest rooms were combined to make nine spacious bedrooms and eight baths. Room was also made for a restaurant, the Squire Jackson's Bar, and a manager's office. The interior is delightfully decorated with auction antiques. Each bedroom has a name above its doorway in a stained-glass transom. Among these are the Bluebonnet

Room, the Pecan Room, and the Alamo Room. The custom hand-quilted bedspreads all coordinated with the period wallpaper give the rooms a homey mood. New plumbing, air-conditioning, and heating were added. So extensive was the renovation that only the slate roof, exterior siding and framing, and interior floors are original.

When you call for reservations, you might want to specify the comfortable three-room, two-bath suite. If you will just be passing through from Houston to San Antonio, stop for breakfast, lunch, or dinner. The chef prepares great fare, ranging from steaks to seafood and country-style potatoes to apple strudel. Breakfast is served on weekends. The soup, salad, and traditional sandwich lunch is served from 11 A.M. to 2 P.M. Wednesday through Sunday, with the traditional dinner served from Thursday through Saturday.

If you like country-and-western dancing, make plans to attend the Knights of Columbus Hall dance held on Saturday night. Also plan to visit the unique Texas towns of Fayetteville, LaGrange (of "The Best Little Whorehouse in Texas" fame), and Columbus.

As for Weimar, it has a charm all its own. Founded in 1873, it was named after the quaint town of Weimar, Germany, by one of its founders, T. W. Pierce. It's a curious fact that at the time the city was built, there were no German immigrants living in the vicinity. It wasn't until much later that Germans began to settle in town. At any rate, you'll love the city park adjacent to the Weimar Country Inn property. Also note the new antique-like bandstand just built for summer concerts.

Country-Style Potatoes

Serves 4 to 6

2 pounds potatoes, peeled and quartered
¼ cup butter or margarine
1 medium onion, chopped
3 slices bacon, chopped
Salt and pepper to taste
Cheddar cheese, grated

Preheat oven to 350°. Boil potatoes until tender. Drain water, chop potatoes into small pieces, and add butter. Fry chopped onion and bacon; then mix with potatoes. Place potato mixture in pan; add salt and pepper. Sprinkle top with cheese, and bake until heated through and cheese is melted.

Breast of Chicken Marinade

Yields 3½ cups

⅓ cup lemon or lime juice
2 tablespoons dry mustard
¼ teaspoon salt
1 tablespoon pepper
½ cup wine vinegar
¼ cup Lea & Perrins Worcestershire sauce
1½ cups salad oil
½ cup soy sauce
Sprinkle of Accent seasoning
Pinch garlic powder

Combine all ingredients. Marinate chicken breasts for several hours. Cook on grill or charbroiler. This marinade turns plain chicken into a tasty and different entrée.

Poppy Seed Salad Dressing

Yields 2½ cups

1 cup sugar
½ teaspoon salt
1 teaspoon dry mustard
1½ teaspoons paprika
½ cup vinegar
1½ cups salad oil
1 teaspoon onion
2 tablespoons poppy seeds

Mix sugar, salt, dry mustard, paprika, and vinegar together thoroughly. Add oil gradually, beating constantly. Add onion and poppy seeds; shake to mix thoroughly. This is great on fruit salad as well as on spinach, mandarin orange, and red onion salad.

White House
Goliad

T he date was February 1836. Bowie and Travis were desperately defending the Alamo while Colonel James Walker Fannin, a West Point dropout, was camped at Goliad with four hundred men. Bonham rode from the besieged mission four times to plead with Fannin to come to their aid, yet Bonham met with a refusal each time.

At last, on February 28, Fannin decided to take most of his men to San Antonio but mysteriously turned around and came back to Goliad. The Alamo fell, and General Sam Houston ordered Fannin to retreat. Fannin was a monument of indecision. He buried his guns, started to retreat, then returned and dug them up. Finally, on March 18, Fannin complied with Houston's orders, but it was too late. Attacked and defeated by General Urrea, the Colonel surrendered on the promise of honorable treatment.

When General Santa Anna rescinded Urrea's promise, Fannin and his men were shot, their bodies burned and tossed into a common grave. For the Texas Centennial, a handsome monument was erected in memory of the lives sacrificed for Texas.

Goliad is a lovely old rural town filled with historic sites. You can travel back to the Spanish mission days at La Bahia, remember the fight for Texas independence at Fannin State Park, or relive the stormy days before the Civil War with the Cart War of 1857. This squabble between Mexican and Texas teamsters resulted in bodies dangling from the Hanging Tree on Goliad's square.

With all of its history, it is no wonder that Goliad appealed to Ruby Mennich as the perfect place for a country inn. This sturdy old home was built in 1935 by the widow of W. O. Huggins, a Texas lawyer of note and editor of the *Houston Chronicle*. The old steam radiators still clank out a cozy heat on chilly days.

The White House offers three charming guest rooms, each with its own bath. While the furnishings are not antiques, they are homey and comfortable. A favorite of the three is the one Ruby has converted from the old servants' quarters downstairs and off the main house. This love-ly retreat offers a maximum of privacy.

Ruby is well known around Goliad for her fabulous cooking, and her catering is always in demand. The White House dining-room table often groans with good food for special parties. For her guests in the inn, Ruby serves a memorable breakfast, which is included in the price of the room. Whether you want a hearty meal to start your day, or just to nibble on a piece of dry toast, you are seated in the dining room with crisp white linens and silver serving pieces.

Managers Jan and Mert Rawson are always on hand to make you feel welcome, and Jan keeps the kitchen filled with the aroma of something delicious baking in the oven.

Egg Casserole

Serves 6

6 eggs, beaten
2 cups milk
½ cup cheddar cheese, grated
Dash salt
6 slices white sandwich bread, cubed

Mix beaten eggs with milk, cheese, and salt. Pour over cubed bread in lightly greased 8-inch or 9-inch square baking dish. Refrigerate over-night. The next morning, beat mixture with fork and leave at room temperature. (Baking time will depend on temperature of eggs.) Bake at 350° approximately 30 minutes. Cut in squares to serve.

A variation on this recipe involves leaving out the milk and spicing it up a bit. Line baking dish with thin or thick slices of jalapeño peppers (depending upon the condition of your stomach). After baking, cut in-to bite-sized pieces and serve as an appetizer or snack.

Wise
Manor
Jefferson

Historic Jefferson has more than its share of charm and hospitality, and one of the greatest proponents of these traditions is Katherine Ramsay Wise. Katherine's inn is the quaint two-story salmon and white gabled cottage on Houston Street. You can't miss it, for Old Glory is waving in the East Texas breeze among pecan trees five centuries old. Open the wrought iron gate and enter the wonderful world of Wise Manor.

Wise Manor is filled with family possessions, among which are an abundance of oil paintings of Katherine's ancestors. Great-great-grandfather, great-grandmother, grandfather, and grandmother share the walls with Katherine's mother and father and her own daughters and granddaughters. Seven generations of portraits grace this lovely old home.

Built in 1851, Wise Manor is in the oldest part of Jefferson. During the Civil War, Yankees were imprisoned in the stockade near the house, and later southern political prisoners took the soldiers' place during Reconstruction. A few blocks down, travelers entered Jefferson from San Augustine on the Big Cypress ferry, so lots of horses, buggies, and wagons passed Wise Manor in those years.

J. M. Dollehite was the first resident of this old house; then Mrs. Ernestine Stern made it her home. In 1929 two native Jeffersonians returned home and purchased the cottage; they were Asa E. and Julia Ballauf Ramsay, Katherine's parents. No wonder Katherine takes such pride in her heritage.

Chicken Salad

Serves 4

2 cups white meat of cooked chicken, cubed
1 orange, sectioned
¼ cup white grapes, cut in half
¼ cup salted almonds, halved
1 banana, cut up
¾ cup mayonnaise

Mix together well and chill.

Macaroon Pie

Serves 8

14 saltine crackers, rolled fine (be sure to count each square as one)
12 dates, chopped fine
½ cup pecans, chopped fine
1 cup sugar
3 egg whites, beaten until stiff
¾ teaspoon salt
1 generous teaspoon almond extract

Combine cracker crumbs, dates, pecans, and sugar. Beat egg whites stiff, gradually adding salt and almond extract. Fold in first mixture. Bake in buttered 9-inch pie pan for 45 minutes at 300°. (There's no pie crust to this one.) Serve with whipped cream or ice cream with cherry on top.

Note: If you decide to double this recipe, multiply all proportions by two except the salt. Use only 1 teaspoon and bake in a 10-inch by 15½-inch pan.

Spinach Casserole

Serves 5

    2 packages frozen spinach, cooked
    ½ cup liquid reserved from spinach
    1 5⅓-ounce can evaporated milk
    ½ teaspoon garlic salt
    ½ teaspoon celery salt
    1 tablespoon flour
    ⅓ 8-ounce roll jalapeño cheese

Mix together all ingredients except flour, spinach, and cheese. Heat mixture until hot; then add flour to thicken. Add cheese and heat until it is fully melted. Line dish with cooked spinach and pour hot mixture over the top. Bake 25 minutes in a 250° oven.

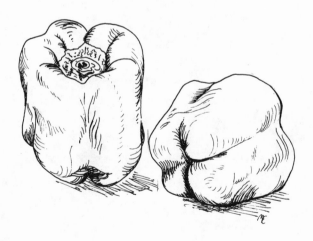

Yacht Club Hotel
Port Isabel

If you have priced real estate on South Padre Island recently, you may find it incredible that its first owner picked up the entire Isla de Corpus Christi for a measly 400 pesos. Padre Nicolas Balli acquired all of this prime real estate about 1800 from a generous Charles IV of Spain when Texas was Spanish property. Of course, all the good padre got was a lot of salt grass, mosquitoes, and cannibalistic Karankawa Indians who liked human flesh as much as the mosquitoes did. But it was from the good padre that the island acquired its present name.

Port Isabel did not come into being until the Mexican War, when General Zachary Taylor needed a base of supplies for Fort Brown. When the war ended, the forty-niners arrived on their way to the elusive California gold fields, and Port Isabel became one of the busiest harbors on the Texas Coast. In 1936 Brownsville completed its deep-water port and killed Port Isabel's main source of income.

Tourists have rediscovered this historic little port, and one of their favorite attractions is the lighthouse, now a state park. The light's welcome beam first greeted ships in 1853, and during the Civil War it was a highly coveted prize by Union and Confederate troops. The Yankees won, of course, and it was at Port Isabel that Lew Wallace arrived (before he wrote *Ben Hur*) with his scheme of offering the Confederates amnesty if they would join with the United States in ousting the French from Mexico. The die-hard Rebels were just not interested. The light went out in 1905, but when it became a state park, the lighthouse once again appeared on sea charts.

Another major attraction in Port Isabel is the grand old Yacht Club Hotel. Back in 1926, a group of prominent Rio Grande Valley businessmen formed a corporation to build a private club worthy of their social status. Naturally, the Yacht Club was the center of the Valley's high-society events. When the crash came in 1929, such luxuries as private clubs were wiped out, along with the members' fortunes. Luckily, the building was saved when multimillionaire John H. Shary bought out the original members and opened the club to the public. The Yacht Club's fine restaurant soon became *the* place to dine on seafood brought in from Texas waters.

The wear and tear of time finally closed the hotel in 1969, when renovation became an absolute necessity. Now reopened for several years, the Yacht Club is still making improvements. In addition to adding new plumbing and air-conditioning, refurbishing the rooms, and sprucing up the facade, the owners have installed a swimming pool that enhances the tropical grounds. Yet the Yacht Club retains its special aura. The mammoth hotel crest was specially carved in Madrid by Antonio Navidad and Baltazar Hervas, who have worked as a team since 1966. Best of all, the food is once again making the Yacht Club *the* place to dine.

High beamed ceilings, stark white walls, red carpets, velvet draperies, and handmade Mexican furniture dominated by a huge fireplace create a beautiful atmosphere in which to enjoy cocktails and magnificent seafood. The recipe for the best stuffed crab in the world is a house secret, and no wonder. This dish has won top honors in seafood preparation. Also on the predominantly seafood menu are flounder, scallops, shrimp, lobster, Alaskan King Crab, oysters, and broiled red snapper. If you find it hard to choose which dish you prefer, just wait until you read the extensive wine list. During the season, you may have to take a reservation as early as 6 P.M. to have dinner at this extremely popular restaurant. Take whatever time you can get. It will be well worth it for a memorable meal.

Broiled Red Snapper

Serves 4

Bob Speir, co-owner of the Yacht Club, says that a fresh red snapper will be odorless and that the key to good broiled fish is its freshness. Here's how he prepares this popular dish.

4 8-ounce snapper filets
Melted butter
Paprika
Season-all

Arrange filets in a shallow baking dish; butter generously; season with paprika and Season-all. Bake at 500° for 5 minutes or until done. Serve at once with a good tartar sauce made with chopped onion, dill relish, sweet relish, and mayonnaise.

Spinach Salad

Serves 4

5 ounces salad oil
2 ounces red wine vinegar
¾ teaspoon sugar
1 ounce brandy
Spinach (enough for four individual salads)
3 tablespoons fresh bacon bits or Oscar Meyer's Real Bacon Bits
Chopped egg for garnish

Heat first three ingredients in a shallow pan until simmered. Add brandy, and flame to burn alcohol. Allow to cool and then pour liquid over spinach. Toss. Divide spinach into salad plates and top with bacon bits. Garnish with the chopped egg.

Index